200 great

hamlyn | **all colour gardening**

200 great containers

Joanna Smith

An Hachette Livre UK Company
www.hachettelivre.co.uk

First published in Great Britain in 2009 by Hamlyn,
a division of Octopus Publishing Group Ltd
2–4 Heron Quays, London E14 4JP
www.octopusbooks.co.uk

ISBN 978-0-600-61848-5

A CIP catalogue record for this book is available
from the British Library

Printed and bound in China

1 2 3 4 5 6 7 8 9 10

contents

introduction

introduction

Containers are the ultimate in instant gardening. In just a few hours it is possible to create a number of different container displays, and that includes a trip to the nursery or garden centre to buy the ingredients. And if you choose the containers and plants well, they look good immediately and can transform your patio area, creating a big visual impact.

Containers are also the ultimate in easy-care gardening. There is no digging involved, no problems with encroaching perennial weeds, and as the plants are not at ground level there is less back-breaking bending. It is also easier to tend plants when they are growing in a container as you can control the moisture, nutrients and soil and give them the conditions they like best.

There are two types of container display. First, there are the permanent plantings that stay the same throughout the year – for example, a handsome evergreen shrub underplanted with herbaceous perennials to add summer colour. Then there are the temporary displays designed for a specific season, using only plants that are at their best at that moment. Permanent plantings involve less work and can look good all year, but temporary displays allow more scope in terms of creativity, and you can be experimental as you'll only have to live with the results for a short while.

This book contains 200 ideas for great permanent and temporary container displays, from flower-filled hanging baskets of summer bedding to year-round containers of shrubs and perennials. They feature a wide range of different plants, from all the summer favourites, such as pelargoniums and petunias, to grasses, vegetables and some rather more exotic subjects. Use the ideas as recipes to be followed carefully or as inspiration to create your own unique combinations. But most of all just enjoy yourself – you can always change it if you don't like it.

KEY TO SYMBOLS

site in full sun

requires plenty of watering

site in partial shade

requires moderate water

site in shade

feed regularly

frost hardy

requires extra care

frost tender

choosing containers

Containers come in lots of different shapes and sizes, but as long as they hold compost they are suitable for accommodating plants. There are a few practical and aesthetic pointers to help you choose.

size

The size of the container will largely be dictated by the position in which it is going to stand: it needs to be in scale with its surroundings. On the whole, fewer larger containers work better in a space than lots of little ones as larger containers have more presence. In addition, of course, they are easier to tend as they contain a larger volume of compost, requiring less frequent feeding and watering.

material

The material you choose – terracotta, glazed, wooden, galvanized – will partly depend on the style of the surroundings, whether sleek and contemporary or traditional cottage garden. However, there are also practical considerations to take into account. The main one is whether a pot is porous or not: the soil in a terracotta pot dries out quickly, making it impracticable for moisture-loving plants like hostas but perfect for alpines, which hate wet soil. You can line porous containers with plastic to help them retain moisture. Wooden planters will rot unless they are protected, so either use a plastic liner or treat the wood with a water-repellent product. They will still, however, have a limited life.

shape

The main thing to consider when choosing the shape of a container is the volume of compost it contains: the less compost the more work. Here are a few things to keep in mind:

• Shallow bowls contain less compost than deeper tubs.

• Troughs and windowboxes tend to be quite narrow and shallow, so they don't hold a lot of compost and have to be watered and fed more frequently.

• Hanging baskets also hold relatively little compost, and unless they are lined with plastic or have a rigid plastic base they also dry out extremely quickly.

composts

The type and quality of compost can make the difference between success and failure, between healthy, bushy plants covered with flowers and a disappointing show with weak, stunted foliage and few blooms.

types of compost
There are two main types of compost available: those that contain soil and those that don't.

Soil-based composts are designed for permanent plantings as they are heavy (offering good anchorage) and free-draining (allowing good aeration). The nutrients are released slowly, and they have a good structure, which withstands the test of time.

Soil-less composts, usually based on peat, are designed for temporary plant displays. They are light and easy to use, but the structure breaks down quite quickly, and they soon decrease in volume. They do not hold nutrients well, so you have to feed more often, and they are prone to waterlogging in wet weather and dry out quickly in dry weather.

When planting a container with a temporary display, it is a good idea to use a 50:50 mixture of soil-based and soil-less compost to reap the benefits of both and make life easier. The soil-based compost provides good drainage and stability, while the soil-less compost makes the mixture more moisture-retentive. Try to find a peat-free soil-less compost, an environmentally-friendly product that does not encourage the depletion of peat beds.

Ericaceous (acidic) composts are soil-based composts formulated for growing acid-loving plants such as rhododendrons and heathers. These plants will not grow well in multi-purpose composts.

extra ingredients
Some plants do best with a little extra care. Ferns and hostas, for example, thrive in moist compost so will benefit if you add some well-rotted manure or garden compost to the compost in the tub to improve water-retention. A third by volume is about right.

Alpines and succulent plants, on the other hand, prefer an extremely free-draining compost, so it is a good idea to add about a third by volume of sharp horticultural grit to a standard potting compost to improve the drainage.

all-important drainage
It is vital to get the compost right, but you also need to check that moisture can drain adequately out of the container. Check that your tub has sufficient drainage holes in the bottom, and if there aren't enough make some more with a drill.

planting a container

No matter what type of tub, compost and plants you have, the basic method for planting a container is the same. It is worth spending a little time to give your plants the best possible start.

1 Start by watering the plants thoroughly to make sure their rootballs are moist right through. Place pebbles or pieces of broken flowerpot over the drainage holes in the bottom of the tub to prevent the compost from being washed out. Start filling the tub with compost, firming lightly as you go. Stand the largest plant, still in its pot, on the compost to check the level: the top of the rootball should come about 4 cm (1½ in) below the rim of the tub. Adjust the compost if necessary.

2 Plan your arrangement with the plants still in their pots. Move them around until you are happy with the layout. If it's a temporary display, arrange the plants close together to give maximum impact straight away. If it's a permanent planting, space the plants so they have room to grow. When you are happy, start removing the plants from their pots by turning the pots upside down while supporting the compost with your fingers, which will be either side of the plant.

3 Add more compost to the tub, packing it lightly round the rootballs as you go and firming gently. The plants should end up with the tops of their rootballs level with the top of the compost. Firm the compost lightly between the plants to check for any gaps. Aim for the top of the compost to come 4 cm (1½ in) below the pot rim to allow room for watering.

4 Add a layer of horticultural grit or gravel if you like. This will suppress weeds, help retain moisture and add a finishing touch, especially important if there is bare compost visible between the plants. Water the tub thoroughly using a watering can fitted with a fine rose. This will prevent the compost from being displaced as you water.

planting a hanging basket

There are two types of hanging basket: those with solid sides, which are planted in the same way as any other container, and those with open sides through which plants can grow. Here's how to plant the latter.

1 First line the basket to prevent the compost falling out. You can use moss, cocoa fibre or synthetic fibre, all of which are built up in layers as you fill the basket; or a one-piece liner, such as hessian, moulded paper or a specially designed hanging basket liner through which you need to make holes for the plants. Place a small saucer in the bottom of the basket to help retain moisture.

2 Place a little compost in the bottom of the basket and start positioning the lowest layer of plants, feeding the foliage through the holes in the sides of the basket from inside out. Add more compost as necessary, firming it around the rootballs of the plants, then start on the next row of plants higher up the basket sides. Continue up the sides of the basket.

3 When the basket is full, plant the last few plants in the compost in the top and firm lightly to make sure there are no air gaps. Try to make the compost in the centre of the basket slightly lower than that at the sides to make watering easier. Water the basket thoroughly using a watering can fitted with a fine rose.

4 Insert fertilizer spikes or pellets into the top of the compost if you like. These release nutrients slowly and help make sure the plants are well fed. Hanging baskets contain a lot of plants for the volume of compost so this is a good idea.

siting containers

There are both practical and aesthetic considerations to be taken into account when siting containers, so think carefully before you position them.

pleasing the plants

Unless you have chosen plants to suit the position of an existing container, you will need to position your container where the plants will thrive. Shade-loving plants will obviously need a shady position and sun-worshippers a sunny one, but also bear in mind whether the spot is sheltered or exposed to cold winds, the worst of the winter wet or heavy frosts. Buildings can channel winds in unlikely directions, and some plants will not do well in a continual draught.

pleasing the eye

Position is everything when it comes to getting the maximum visual impact out of your containers.

• Small containers, or those with small, intricate plants, should be placed where they can be appreciated at close quarters. Site them on a table on the patio, on top of a low wall, on a plinth, on a doorstep or just somewhere you pass by often.

• Larger tubs can play many different roles in the overall design of your garden or patio. Use them as focal points to add drama –

perhaps standing a container at the point where two paths cross or at the end of a vista to create a full stop. They can also be used in pairs to frame a doorway, archway or even an attractive view.

• Containers are also the perfect solution for softening an otherwise austere feature like a plain stretch of fence, a bare house wall or a large expanse of patio. Place a large tub overflowing with foliage and flowers there and it becomes a garden.

• A handsome plant in a container can also be used to draw the eye away from an ugly feature like a dull shed, oil tank or compost bin. It doesn't need to the hide the feature; just having it nearby will divert attention.

• Containers can also be used to enhance flights of steps. Use a series of identical containers, one to a step on each side, to frame the steps and add drama, or cluster small groups of little pots at the sides of the steps to add interest and soften the effect.

• A pair of large containers is perfect for framing a feature such as a doorway, gateway or arch to emphasize it.

• When positioning, think about whether to group your containers or use them singly. A single, large container has a more dramatic presence and works well as a design feature in its own right. A group of pots has a more informal look.

container care

Caring for plants growing in containers is much like caring for plants in beds and borders, but it is important to bear in mind that they rely on you for moisture and nutrients because they cannot draw them from the surrounding soil.

feeding

The nutrient requirements of plants vary enormously.

• Shrubs and perennials in tubs with a fair amount of compost will be happy with a dose of slow-release fertilizer each year. Fork a little bonemeal or a granular fertilizer into the top of the compost in spring.

• Annuals, fast-growing perennials grown for their flowers and vegetables will need regular feeding to encourage strong growth and a succession of blooms or fruits. Liquid fertilizers are convenient to use: simply add the required measure to the water when you are watering. Alternatively, do it automatically by inserting fertilizer spikes into the compost when you plant. They release nutrients slowly over a number of weeks.

watering

Even when it rains, container plants receive little moisture so you need to get in the habit of regular watering. Here are a few pointers to make it easier:

• Consider installing an automatic watering system with a timer if you have lots of containers but little spare time.

• Add moisture-retaining gel crystals to the compost when you plant if there is going to be lots of plants in a small space.

• Make sure the level of the compost is at least 2.5 cm (1 in) below the rim of the container so you can really soak the compost when you water.

• Stand pots in saucers. It really helps to conserve moisture.

deadheading

Removing the dead blooms of annuals and most perennials as they fade is vital if you want to encourage them to produce more. As soon as an annual sets seed its job is done, so it stops flowering and dies. Keep deadheading and give them a reason to produce more flowers.

repotting

Plants growing in containers for more than a year or two will need to be repotted when they outgrow their space. Simply remove them from the current pot, gently break up the outer edges of the rootball to remove some of the old compost and repot into fresh compost, using a slightly larger container if necessary.

spring collection

spring beauties

You need

20 *Tulipa* 'Angélique' bulbs **A**

5 *Myosotis sylvatica*
(forget-me-not) **B**

A dazzling array of lovely pastel pink tulips and soft blue forget-me-nots in a half-barrel is the very essence of spring.

Planting & care Plant the half-barrel in autumn. Fill it to 20 cm (8 in) below the rim with a free-draining compost. Arrange the tulip bulbs on top of the compost with the pointed ends uppermost. Add another 15 cm (6 in) of compost on top and firm lightly. Plant the forget-me-nots, evenly spaced, in the top of the tub. Keep the compost just moist. After flowering, feed the bulbs with a liquid fertilizer to plump them up for next year. Remove the forget-me-nots and replace them with summer bedding.

Or you could try a cool and elegant all-white display with white forget-me-nots and white tulips, such as the simple 'Purissima', the green-based 'Spring Green' or the frilly 'White Parrot'.

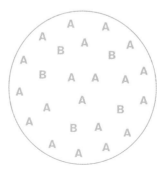

beautiful ballerinas

You need

5 *Tulipa* 'Queen of Night' bulbs **A**

15 *Tulipa* 'Ballerina' bulbs **B**

2 *Skimmia japonica* cultivars **C**

3 *Hedera helix* cultivars (variegated ivy) **D**

3 *Pennisetum alopecuroides* 'Hameln' (fountain grass) **E**

Vibrant orange tulip 'Ballerina' is shown to good advantage against a backdrop of pinky skimmia and the brown winter foliage of spiky fountain grass. This container is designed to be viewed from one side only, perfect for positioning in front of a hedge, fence or wall.

Planting & care Plant the tub in autumn using a free-draining container compost. Fill the tub to 20 cm (8 in) below the rim and arrange the bulbs on top of the compost, pointed ends up. Add another 15 cm (6 in) of compost, firm lightly and plant the other plants in the top. Keep just moist over winter, then water regularly in spring and summer. Feed in early summer after the bulbs have flowered.

Or you could try cream-coloured daffodils, such as 'Canisp' or 'Cool Crystal', instead of the tulips for a more muted display.

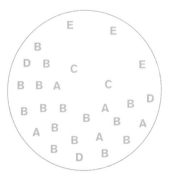

primrose basket

You need

3 *Primula* Wanda Supreme
   Series (primroses) **A**

8 *Crocus* 'Vanguard'
   (Dutch crocus) bulbs **B**

This pretty woven wall basket is overflowing with dainty lilac crocuses and pink primroses, perfect for cheering up a plain wall in early spring. Plant up a number of baskets and hang them close together for a fuller display.

Planting & care Plant the basket in autumn. Line it with polythene sheeting and make a drainage hole in the bottom. Fill with free-draining compost and plant the primroses in the top. Use a stick to make holes between the primroses for the bulbs: they should be planted about 5 cm (2 in) below the surface, pointed ends up. Cover with more compost and keep moist over winter. After the flowers have finished, plant out the crocuses and primroses in the garden and fill the basket with summer bedding.

Or you could try a summer display of ivy-leaved pelargoniums in the basket, which would thrive in the dry conditions a small amount of compost provides. 'L'Elégante' has white flowers and lovely silvery foliage with cream and pink variegations.

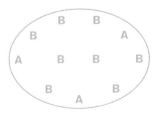

basket of bulbs

You need

10 *Tulipa* 'Stresa' bulbs **A**

30 *Crocus ancyrensis*
  bulbs **B**

A simple rattan hanging basket is filled with golden crocuses and smart yellow and red tulip 'Stresa', bringing a ray of sunshine and a cheerful note to the garden in early spring.

Planting & care Plant the hanging basket in autumn. Line it with a piece of polythene and make some holes in it. Fill to within 15 cm (6 in) of the rim with a free-draining container compost, then arrange the tulip bulbs, pointed ends up, on top. Add another 8 cm (3 in) of compost and arrange the crocus bulbs around the edges of the basket. Fill the basket with compost to within 2.5 cm (1 in) of the rim and firm lightly. Keep just moist over winter. After the bulbs have finished flowering, plant them out in the garden and fill the basket with bedding plants.

Or you could try a pink and purple planting scheme with deep pink tulip 'Pink Diamond' and purple-pink crocus 'Ruby Giant'.

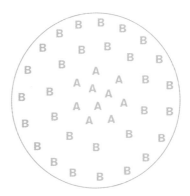

the scent of spring

You need

10 *Narcissus* 'Bridal Crown' (daffodil) bulbs **A**

6 *Viola* cultivars (pansy) **B**

4 *Hedera helix* cultivars (ivy) **C**

A simple terracotta pot is ideal to enhance a gorgeous group of 'Bridal Crown' daffodils, with their intoxicating scent. Cream pansies and cream-splashed ivy soften the effect.

Planting & care Plant the tub in autumn, using a free-draining container compost. Fill the tub to within 20 cm (8 in) of the rim and arrange the daffodils on top, pointed ends up. Add 15 cm (6 in) of compost and firm lightly, then plant the pansies and ivy in the top. Keep moist over winter, and apply a liquid feed when the daffodils finish flowering. Remove the pansies when they finish flowering and replace with summer bedding. Plant new pansies in the tub the following autumn.

Or you could try replacing the pansies with pretty white *Anemone blanda* (windflower). Plant the bulbs about 5 cm (2 in) below the surface of the compost.

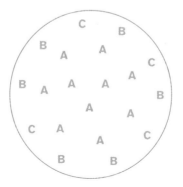

double the pleasure

You need

10 *Tulipa* 'Blue Diamond'
bulbs **A**

1 *Euphorbia amygdaloides*
'Purpurea' (spurge) **B**

1 *Phlomis italica* **C**

1 *Viola* 'Magnifico' **D**

1 *Hedera helix* cultivar (ivy) **E**

1 *Polemonium caeruleum*
'Brise d'Anjou' (variegated
Jacob's ladder) **F**

1 *Corydalis flexuosa*
'Purple Leaf' **G**

This lovely container of perennials, annuals and
bulbs for late spring includes gorgeous double
tulips, bright green euphorbia, silvery felted
phlomis and blue corydalis, an intricate mix
of colours, textures and forms.

Planting & care Plant the tub in autumn using a free-
draining container compost. Fill the tub to 20 cm (8 in)
below the rim, then arrange the tulip bulbs on top of the
compost, pointed ends up. Add more compost, to just
below the pot rim, and plant the other plants in the top.
Keep just moist over winter. Apply a liquid fertilizer when
the tulip flowers fade. The phlomis and polemonium will
go on to flower in the summer, so keep watering regularly
and enjoy a second show.

Or you could try replacing the tulips with ornamental
onion bulbs, which flower a little later. *Allium caeruleum*
has bright blue, rounded flower heads, while *A.
rosenbachianum* has gorgeous deep purple flowers.

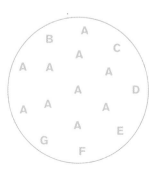

spring cheer

You need

15 *Tulipa* 'Peach Blossom' bulbs **A**

15 *Narcissus* (daffodil) bulbs **B**

15 *Primula vulgaris* cultivars (bedding primroses) **C**

4 *Scilla siberica* (squill) bulbs **D**

This bright and cheerful windowbox display of primroses and spring bulbs in a range of vivid colours will certainly blow away the cobwebs.

Planting & care Plant the windowbox in autumn using a free-draining container compost. Fill the box to 15 cm (6 in) below the rim and arrange the tulip and daffodil bulbs on top. Add another 12.5 cm (5 in) of compost, firm lightly and plant the primroses in the top. Make 5 cm (2 in) deep holes with your finger and pop in the scilla bulbs, pointed ends up. Refill the holes. Keep the compost just moist over winter. After the plants have finished flowering, transplant the bulbs and primroses to the garden.

Or you could try an all-yellow windowbox display, using yellow tulips, such as the double-flowered 'Monte Carlo' or the elegant single 'Sweet Harmony', with sunny yellow daffodils and all yellow primroses.

B	A	B	B	C	B	A	B	B	A	B	A	B
C	C	A	A	B	C	C	A	B	A	B	C	A
A	B	C	C	C	B	A	C	C	A	C		
C	C	A	D	A	B	D	D	C	D	B	A	

cheeky faces

You need

10 *Viola* (mixed smaller
flowered viola) **A**

A visit to the garden centre in spring will reveal a whole range of cute little violas, with faces of all colours. Pick a selection of your favourites and plant them in a simple terracotta bowl, which won't detract from their pretty colours and intricate markings.

Planting & care Plant the violas in spring in a free-draining container compost and place the tub in sun or partial shade. Water and feed regularly to keep the violas going: they should provide a colourful display right through the spring and summer. Remove and discard the plants when they become long and straggly and produce fewer flowers, or shear off the foliage, feed and water well and wait for them to shoot again.

Or you could try filling the bowl with heartsease (*Viola tricolor*), the wild pansy, for a simpler cottage-garden look. The flowers have pretty little yellow, deep purple and white faces.

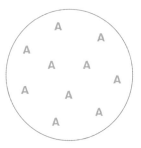

cool cream and white

You need

1 *Helleborus niger* (Christmas rose) **A**

5 *Hyacinthus orientalis* 'City of Haarlem' (hyacinth) bulbs **B**

1 *Acorus gramineus* 'Ogon' (Japanese rush) **C**

1 *Silene uniflora* 'Druett's Variegated' (variegated sea campion) **D**

2 *Erica carnea* 'Springwood White' (heather) **E**

This sophisticated early spring display uses white heathers and a hellebore with creamy hyacinths. The flowers are enhanced by the variegated foliage of Japanese rush and sea campion, a great combination of shapes and patterns in a muted colour range.

Planting & care Plant the tub in autumn using a free-draining, moisture-retentive compost. The hyacinth bulbs should be planted about 10 cm (4 in) below the surface of the compost. Keep just moist over winter. Feed with a liquid fertilizer in mid-spring as the hyacinth flowers fade. All these plants are perennial and can be kept in the container from year to year. The sea campion produces lovely white flowers in summer.

Or you could try a display of blue, white and grey, using *Silene uniflora* 'Robin Whitebreast' with grey-green foliage, *Festuca glauca* (blue fescue) instead of the Japanese rush, and deep blue hyacinths, such as 'Delft Blue' or 'Blue Jacket'.

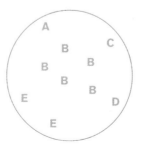

pink perfection

You need

10 double late tulip bulbs,
 such as 'Angélique' or
 'Maywonder' **A**

8 pink bedding ranunculus **B**

A lovely weathered terracotta trough contains
gorgeous blousy peony-flowered tulips and
wonderful deep pink ranunculus – a simple
but effective display for late spring.

Planting & care Plant the trough in autumn using free-
draining, moisture-retentive compost. Fill the trough to
15 cm (6 in) below the rim with compost and arrange the
tulip bulbs on top, pointed ends up. Add another 10 cm
(4 in) of compost and firm lightly. Plant the ranunculus
plants in the top, arranged along the front of the trough.
Keep the compost just moist over winter. Feed with a
liquid fertilizer when the tulips have finished flowering.
Discard the ranunculus when they stop flowering and
plant the tulips out in the garden.

Or you could try a more vibrant display of bright orange
or yellow ranunculus with tulip 'Golden Artist', a rich
orange tulip with green stripes up the backs of the petals,
or tulip 'Allegretto', a big, bright double tulip with red and
orange flowers.

	A		A		A		A		A
A		A		A		A		A	
		B		B		B			B
B			B		B		B		

citrus shades

Lime green euphorbia and bright orange violas
make a pleasing contrast in a plain and simple
terracotta tub, a zesty combination of colours
for late spring.

Planting & care Plant the tub in autumn or early spring
using a free-draining compost. Choose a bushy euphorbia
plant with a number of stems for a full display, or plant
three smaller plants in the tub. Plant the violas around the
euphorbia, and topdress the pot with a layer of gravel to
set-off the plants and suppress weeds. Keep the compost
just moist and remove the dead flower heads from the
violas to encourage them to produce more flowers.

Or you could try *Euphorbia griffithii* 'Fireglow' with its
bright orange flowers and red-tinged foliage. Choose
orange violas for a harmonious display or clear blue
violas for a striking contrast.

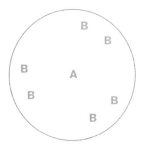

stripy irises

You need

1 *Iris pseudacorus* 'Variegata'
  (yellow flag) **A**

This towering and stately iris makes an elegant subject for a simple green glazed pot. The handsome striped foliage looks good from spring to autumn, while the pretty yellow flowers are a bonus in late spring.

Planting & care Plant the tub at any time of year using a rich, moisture-retentive compost. Mix in some well-rotted garden compost or manure if you can. This iris needs moist, even wet, soil so use a glazed tub to retain moisture and stand it in a saucer of water. As it grows quickly, one plant is enough to fill the tub. Fork in some bonemeal or other slow-release fertilizer each year in early spring.

Or you could try growing another moisture-loving iris, such as *Iris laevigata* with purple flowers, *I. l.* var. *alba* with white flowers or *I. l.* 'Rosea' with pink flowers.

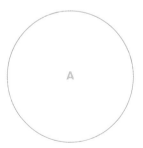

true blue

You need

15 *Muscari armeniacum*
(grape hyacinth) bulbs **A**

3 *Milium effusum* 'Aureum'
(golden wood millet) **B**

True blue grape hyacinths are set off to good advantage by the newly emerging lime green leaves of golden wood millet. As the bulbs die down, the grass will fill the basket with soft, bright foliage through to autumn.

Planting & care Plant the basket in autumn using a moisture-retentive compost. Plant the golden wood millets first, equally spaced in the basket, then poke the muscari bulbs into the compost around them with the convex, more pointed ends up. The bulbs should be about 5 cm (2 in) below the surface of the compost. Keep just moist over winter. Feed with a liquid fertilizer after the bulbs have flowered.

Or you could try growing white grape hyacinths (*Muscari botryoides 'Album'*) underplanted with the black grassy foliage of *Ophiopogon planiscapus* 'Nigrescens'.

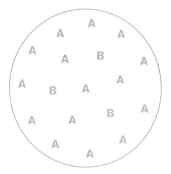

classical elegance

You need

3 *Helleborus orientalis* (lenten rose) **A**

3 *Hyacinthus orientalis* (hyacinth) bulbs **B**

3 *Primula vulgaris* cultivars (bedding primroses) **C**

3 *Hedera helix* cultivars (ivy) **D**

Graceful pink lenten roses rise above cute faded pink primroses and light pink hyacinths in a classical terracotta pot. The rim of the pot has been softened by trails of red-tinged ivy, wrapped loosely around the edges.

Planting & care Plant the pot in autumn using a moisture-retentive compost. Plant the hellebores first, then sink the hyacinth bulbs into the compost between them, pointed ends up, about 10 cm (4 in) deep. Plant the primroses and ivies around the edges of the pot, then wrap the ivy trails loosely around the pot rim. Keep moist over winter, then apply a liquid feed as the plants come into flower. Feed again in early summer and keep the compost just moist.

Or you could try creating the same display in shades of soft yellow, with *Helleborus* x *hybridus* 'Citron', pale yellow primroses and hyacinths, and *Hedera helix* 'Buttercup' with its lovely golden foliage.

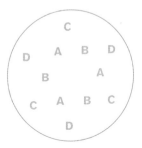

spring sunshine

You need

1 *Ilex aquifolium* (holly) **A**

3 *Lonicera nitida* 'Baggesen's Gold' **B**

3 *Viola* cultivars (pansy) **C**

8 *Tulipa* 'West Point' bulbs **D**

This sunny spring display includes yellow lily-flowered tulips, yellow pansies and golden-leaved lonicera, with holly to add height and structure. Replace the pansies with fresh plants when they finish flowering and you can keep the display going all year.

Planting & care Plant the tub in autumn using a free-draining compost. Arrange the holly in the middle and the three loniceras evenly spaced around the sides. Plant the tulip bulbs in a ring around the holly, pointed ends up and about 10 cm (4 in) deep. Lastly, pop the pansies between the lonicera plants and firm the compost well. Keep the compost just moist and feed with a liquid fertilizer as the tulip flowers fade.

Or you could try a blue and white display with *Ilex aquifolium* 'Argentea Marginata' (a pretty holly with white-edged leaves), green-leaved *Lonicera nitida*, bright white pansies and tulip 'Blue Parrot'.

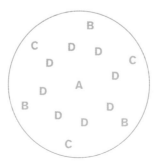

cheerful contrast

You need

6 *Viola* cultivars (pansy) **A**

6 *Anemone blanda* 'Blue Star' (windflower) bulbs **B**

Cheerful orange pansies and bright blue windflowers make a pleasing contrast for early spring. The plain terracotta tub has a distressed turquoise paint finish to enhance the vivid colours of the display.

Planting & care Plant the tub in autumn using a free-draining compost. Fill the tub to 10 cm (4 in) below the rim and arrange the anemone bulbs in a group in the middle on top of the compost. Add another 5 cm (2 in) of compost and plant the pansies equally spaced around the edges of the tub. Keep just moist over winter and apply a liquid feed as the plants come into flower. Discard the pansies when they finish flowering and plant the anemone bulbs in the garden.

Or you could try different contrasting colours, such as white *Anemone blanda* 'White Splendour' with deep purple/black pansies; or bright pink *A. b.* 'Pink Star' with golden yellow pansies, a dazzling combination.

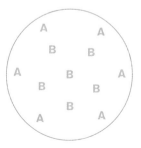

simplicity itself

You need

20 *Viola* cultivars (pansy) **A**

While it's tempting to combine a whole range of different plants in a container, this display proves that understatement can work just as well. There's enough variation in the colour of the pansies to add interest, but they are similar enough to create a harmonious whole.

Planting & care Plant the tub in spring just as the young pansy plants are coming into flower so you can see exactly what colours you have. Choose a range of plants with flowers of a similar colour but with some variation in the shade. Use a free-draining compost and space the plants equally in the container. Keep the compost just moist and feed from time to time with a liquid feed to keep the plants blooming. Removing the spent flower heads will extend the flowering period. Discard the plants when they have finished flowering.

Or you could try an en-masse planting of spring-flowering daisies (*Bellis perennis*) with their charming pompon flowers. Choose all pink or all white flowered plants – the doubles are especially attractive.

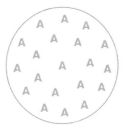

summer stunners

contrasting colours

You need

1 *Helictotrichon sempervirens* (blue oat grass) **A**

2 *Helianthemum* cultivar (rock rose) **B**

2 *Tagetes* cultivar (French marigold) **C**

A pleasing contrast of blue oat grass and orange rock roses and marigolds fills a pretty glazed bowl. This display is best placed in a raised position so the colour and pleasing shape of the bowl can be best appreciated.

Planting & care Plant the container in late spring after all risk of frost has passed using a free-draining compost. Keep the compost on the dry side and apply a liquid fertilizer from time to time throughout the summer to keep the marigolds flowering. Remove the dead marigold flowers as they fade to encourage more to come. Discard the marigolds when they finish flowering. The grass and rock roses are perennials, so transfer them to the garden in autumn or leave them in the bowl and add fresh marigolds next spring.

Or you could try a red and blue display using deep red rock roses and red or mahogany marigolds, such as 'Mars' or 'Red Cherry'.

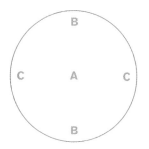

scarlet fire

You need

3 *Pelargonium* Belle Cascade 'Red' (geranium) **A**

2 *Antirrhinum* Bells 'Red' (snapdragon) **B**

3 *Fuchsia* 'Marinka' **C**

8 *Petunia* 'Surfinia Red' **D**

8 *Diascia barberae* 'Ruby Field' **E**

4 *Lobelia* 'Rosamund' **F**

4 *Verbena* Sandy Series 'Red' **G**

4 *Glechoma hederacea* 'Variegata' **H**

This dramatic hanging basket, with its bold array of brilliant red flowers, would make a stunning focal point in any summer garden. For maximum effect, try hanging it on a white wall or against a backdrop of dark green hedging or fencing.

Planting & care Plant the basket in late spring after all risk of frost has passed using a moisture-retentive compost to which you have added some moisture-retaining gel crystals. Insert some fertilizer spikes into the compost because there are a lot of plants in this basket and they will need plenty of nutrients to grow and flower well. Water regularly and remove dead flower heads as they fade to encourage more blooms.

Or you could try using the same plants in a windowbox, where they would cascade gracefully over the sill and down the wall below.

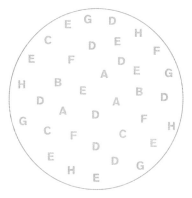

bountiful basket

You need

2 *Petunia* 'Duo' **A**

2 *Nemesia* 'Burning Embers' **B**

1 *Pelargonium* cultivar (geranium) **C**

3 *Viola* cultivar (pansy) **D**

8 *Lobelia erinus* 'Cascade Mixed' **E**

3 *Glechoma hederacea* 'Variegata' **F**

2 *Helichrysum petiolare* 'Variegatum' **G**

This pretty basket contains an unashamed mixture of summer flowers in all shapes and colours. It shows just what can be achieved by disregarding design principles and simply picking what pleases you.

Planting & care Plant the basket in late spring when all risk of frost has passed using a moisture-retentive compost. Insert fertilizer spikes into the compost to feed the plants. Water regularly because baskets dry out quickly. Remove dead flowers as they fade to encourage more blooms throughout the summer.

Or you could try limiting the display to just lobelia 'Cascade Mixed', relying on the different shades of pink, purple, blue and white to add interest. You would need 15–20 plants for a basket of this size.

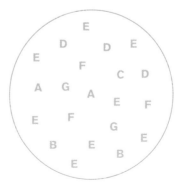

summer sun

You need

1 *Argyranthemum* 'Schone von Nizza' **A**

1 *Tagetes* cultivar (French marigold) **B**

1 *Nemesia* 'Nemesis Orange' **C**

2 *Helichrysum petiolare* 'Silver Mini' **D**

A sunshine yellow windowbox has been planted with a group of sunny plants – argyranthemum with its yellow daisy flowers, French marigold and orange-yellow nemesia. The blue-green foliage makes a pleasing contrast to the yellows.

Planting & care Plant the box in late spring when all risk of frost has passed using a free-draining, moisture-retentive compost. Place in a sunny position and keep the compost just moist. Apply a liquid fertilizer every two weeks while the plants are in flower. Remove the flowers of the marigold and argyranthemum as they fade to encourage the plants to produce more blooms.

Or you could try limiting the colour range even more with a pure yellow nemesia. Team up with lime green *Helichrysum petiolare* 'Limelight'.

dazzling daisies

You need

1 *Argyranthemum* 'Jamaica Primrose' **A**

2 *Verbena* Sandy Series 'Red' **B**

2 *Calibrachoa* Million Bells 'Yellow' **C**

1 *Abutilon* Bella Series **D**

2 *Osteospermum* cultivar **E**

The plain square lines of a terracotta tub are the perfect foil for a full display of tender perennials in shades of red, orange and yellow. With regular deadheading, these plants will flower right through summer and into autumn.

Planting & care Plant the tub in late spring when all risk of frost has passed using a free-draining compost. Keep the compost just moist and apply a liquid fertilizer every two weeks. Deadhead the plants regularly to encourage them to produce more flowers. All these plants are tender perennials so you can either let them die off in the winter and start with fresh plants next spring or move the tub to a frost-free greenhouse to keep them alive. Cut back hard in spring and feed and water well for a repeat performance next summer.

Or you could try combining the same plants in shades of pink, including pale pink *Argyranthemum* 'Vancouver', deep pink *Verbena* 'Sissinghurst', *Calibrachoa* Million Bells 'Pink', *Abutilon* 'Louis Marignac' and *Osteospermum* 'Daisy Mae'.

scarlet spikes

You need

3 *Mimulus* (monkey flower) **A**

2 *Imperata cylindrica*
'Rubra' (Japanese blood
grass) **B**

A colourful combination of scarlet Japanese blood grass and bright yellow mimulus makes a great show in summer. Team up with pots of different grasses for a varied and architectural collection in a sunny spot.

Planting & care Plant the tub in late spring when all risk of frost has passed using a moisture-retentive compost. Stand in a sunny position and water regularly: both plants like moist soil. Remove the flowers from the mimulus as they fade to encourage more blooms to come.

Or you could try replacing the yellow mimulus with a bright red one to match the blood grass. Alternatively, try some of the other handsome grasses, such as zebra grass (*Miscanthus sinensis* 'Zebrinus') with its tall green foliage banded with yellow, the bronze-leaved *Carex flagellifera* or the stripy *Carex oshimensis* 'Evergold', which makes a pretty mound of soft foliage.

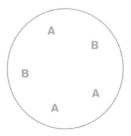

pretty pastels

You need

2 *Salvia farinacea* cultivar (mealy sage) **A**

3 *Campanula carpatica* (bell flowers) **B**

2 *Lobelia erinus* cultivar **C**

1 *Verbena* Sandy Series 'Pink' **D**

A simple white windowbox has been planted with an endearing array of pretty pastel pink and blue tender perennials, which will flower all summer long. Be sure to choose a compact verbena cultivar and an edging lobelia to form neat floriferous mounds.

Planting & care Plant the box in late spring when all risk of frost has passed. Use a moisture-retentive compost and insert some fertilizer spikes to make sure the nutrient levels are kept up to encourage plenty of flowers. Deadhead regularly.

Or you could try an all-blue box using the fan flower (*Scaevola aemula*) instead of the pink verbena. This trailing plant has pretty heads of blue, fan-shaped flowers right through summer and into autumn.

vivid shades

You need

3 *Erysimum* cultivar (perennial wallflower) **A**

2 *Euphorbia amygdaloides* var. *robbiae* (spurge) **B**

2 *Carex oshimensis* 'Evergold' (sedge) **C**

This eye-catching early-summer tub contains a vivid array of bright colours: lime green spurge, stripy yellow sedge and the brilliant flowers of erysimum in vibrant pink, rich orange and yellow all on the same plant.

Planting & care Plant the tub when the wallflowers are available using a free-draining, moisture-retentive compost. Use either one or three wallflowers in the middle of the tub, depending on its size. Trim back the wallflowers after flowering and remove the spurge heads as they start to look untidy. Fork a little bonemeal or other slow-release fertilizer into the top of the compost each spring.

Or you could try a purple wallflower, such as *Erysimum* 'Bowles's Mauve' with the lime green spurge and use a lime green grass, such as golden wood millet (*Milium effusum* 'Aureum') instead of the stripy sedge.

pretty in purple

You need

6 *Verbena* cultivar **A**

3 *Xerochrysum bracteatum* cultivar (strawflower) **B**

3 *Helichrysum petiolare* 'Limelight' **C**

A sea of pretty purple verbena is made more vivid by the contrast of the orange and yellow strawflowers nestling among it and the fiery lotus hanging down from the tub above. Lime green helichrysum lightens the scheme.

Planting & care Plant the tub in late spring when all risk of frost has passed using a free-draining compost. Keep the compost moist and apply a liquid fertilizer every two weeks or so. Deadhead the strawflowers and verbenas regularly to keep the flowers coming.

Or you could try combining grey-leaved *Helichrysum petiolare* with the purple verbena and relacing the strawflowers with a fluffy blue *Ageratum houstonianum* cultivar. Choose a compact variety such as 'Blue Mist' with rich blue flowers.

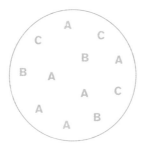

bright begonias

You need

8 *Begonia semperflorens*
   cultivar **A**

2 *Lobelia erinus* cultivar **B**

Bedding begonias are perfect for container displays as they flower all summer long without the need for cosseting. Come rain or shine, they produce their bright flowers in shades of red, pink and white from late spring to autumn.

Planting & care Plant the trough in late spring when all risk of frost has passed using a free-draining, moisture-retentive compost. Place the trough in sun or partial shade and keep the compost moist. Apply a liquid fertilizer every two weeks.

Or you could try an elegant all-white trough using white lobelias and white begonias.

A	A	A	A	A
A	B	A	B	A

cascade of colour

You need

6 *Mimulus aurantiacus* **A**

4 dwarf *Tropaeolum* cultivar
(nasturtium) **B**

3 *Diascia* cultivar **C**

1 *Phygelius* cultivar **D**

1 *Fuchsia* cultivar **E**

3 *Begonia* tubers **F**

1 *Bidens ferulifolia* **G**

1 *Gazania* cultivar **H**

3 *Verbena* cultivar **I**

2 *Pelargonium* cultivar
(geranium) **J**

1 *Lysimachia nummularia*
'Aurea' (creeping Jenny) **K**

A metal manger has been lined with moss
and planted with a cheerful jumble of trailing
summer flowers in warm shades of red, orange
and yellow, a positive profusion of bright flowers
and foliage.

Planting & care Start off the begonia tubers in small
pots indoors in late winter. Plant them one to a pot of
water-retentive compost, stand on a sunny windowsill
and keep moist. Plant the manger in late spring when
all risk of frost has passed. Line it with moss and fill
with water-retentive compost, to which you have added
some moisture-retaining gel crystals. Arrange the plants
in the top and sides of the manger in the same way as
you would when planting a hanging basket. Water the
manger every day as the compost will dry out quickly.

Or you could try growing the same plants in a hanging
basket. All of them have a trailing habit and lend
themselves to baskets.

```
  C   D              C    J        A   C   E
          F    I              H
  B  A                                   F
        B            B   F       A     K      B
  G   A              I    A    I     J      A
```

bronze fountain

You need

1 *Cordyline australis*
(cabbage palm) **A**

4 *Campanula*
portenschlagiana
(Dalmatian bellflower) **B**

A beautiful bronze-leaved palm rises above a sea of blue campanula in a handsome square glazed pot. Although at its best in summer while the campanula is in flower, this container looks good all year round as both of the plants have evergreen foliage.

Planting & care Plant the container at any time of year using a moisture-retentive compost. Place in sun or partial shade and sprinkle a little bonemeal or other slow-release fertilizer into the top of the container each year. Trim off any dead leaves from the palm from time to time, and cut back the campanula if it gets untidy.

Or you could try a variegated palm with cream-striped leaves, such as *Cordyline australis* 'Variegata' or 'Torbay Dazzler', with white bellflowers such as *Campanula carpatica* f. *alba* 'Bressingham White'.

B		B
	A	
B		B

summer beauty

You need

1 *Helichrysum petiolare* 'Rondello' **A**

3 *Scaevola aemula* (fan flower) **B**

2 *Calibrachoa* Celebration 'Fire' **C**

A plain and elegant tub has been planted with trailing tender perennials, forming large mounds of foliage and flowers: the burning pinks and oranges of calibrachoa, lovely purple fan flower and the felted grey foliage of helichrysum.

Planting & care Plant the tub in late spring when all risk of frost has passed using a free-draining compost. Pinch out the growing tips of the plants when they are young to encourage them to branch and form dense mounds. Apply a liquid feed every two weeks and water regularly.

Or you could try combining pink fan flower (*Scaevola* 'Pink Dream') with purple calibrachoa and plain grey *Helichrysum petiolare*.

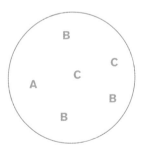

pinks and purples

You need

3 *Pelargonium* 'Frank Headley' **A**

2 *Helichrysum petiolare* **B**

3 *Fuchsia* cultivar **C**

5 *Diascia* cultivar (2 pale pink, 3 red-pink) **D**

10 *Lobelia erinus* cultivar **E**

4 *Glechoma hederacea* 'Variegata' **F**

A white wooden windowbox is overflowing with pretty pastel pinks and purples, including fancy-leaved geraniums with their smart cream and green foliage. A busy, intricate display like this is best viewed against a plain white background.

Planting & care Plant the box in late spring when all risk of frost has passed using a free-draining compost. Be sure to choose trailing lobelia cultivars for a full look. Keep moist and feed regularly with a liquid fertilizer to keep up the display until autumn. Deadhead the pelargoniums to encourage more blooms to come.

Or you could try some of the other handsome fancy-leaved pelargoniums, such as 'Mont Blanc' with its brilliant white, silver and green leaves and white flowers or 'Pink Dolly Varden' with pink flowers and leaves marked with pink, green and cream.

E	A	B	E	A	E	B	A	E
E	D	E	E	D	E	E	D	E
F	C	D	F	C	F	D	C	F

smouldering success

You need

2 *Zinnia elegans*
'Thumbelina' **A**

1 *Tagetes* cultivar (French
marigold) **B**

2 *Verbena* Sandy Series
'Scarlet' **C**

2 *Salvia splendens* (scarlet
sage) **D**

2 *Calibrachoa* Celebration
'Fire' **E**

Instead of following the usual colour rules, this
yellow box has been planted with pinks, oranges
and reds, a clashing blend of rich smouldering
colours that combine beautifully.

Planting & care Plant the box in late spring when all
risk of frost has passed using a free-draining, moisture-
retentive compost. Keep moist and apply a liquid fertilizer
every two weeks. Remove the blooms as they fade to
encourage more to appear.

Or you could try replacing the calibrachoa and verbena
with *Lantana camara*, a lovely spreading plant rather
like a verbena. The flowers heads are a heady mix of
shocking pink and orange, perfect to combine with other
hot colours.

fresh greens

You need

1 *Cotinus coggygria* 'Golden Spirit' (smoke bush) **A**

1 *Helenium* 'The Bishop' **B**

1 *Lysimachia nummularia* 'Aurea' (creeping Jenny) **C**

1 *Lamium maculatum* 'Golden Anniversary' (deadnettle) **D**

1 *Saxifraga* x *urbium* (London pride) **E**

1 *Hakonechloa macra* 'Alboaurea' **F**

A lovely mixture of perennials and a shrub adorns a vivid blue glazed tub. The fresh greens and yellows contrast perfectly with the container, creating a bright and striking diplay for a shady corner in summer.

Planting & care Plant the tub at any time of year using a moisture-retentive compost. Fork a little bonemeal or other slow-release fertilizer into the top of the compost each spring. To maintain a show of vivid lime green foliage, cut back all of the smoke bush stems to one or two buds from the base in early spring each year. Heleniums flower for a long period in summer and can be encouraged further by deadheading. Trim any dead foliage off the deadnettle, London pride and grass in early spring to keep them neat.

Or you could try a similar scheme in purples and reds, including a purple-leaved smoke bush (*Cotinus coggygria* 'Royal Purple'), dark red *Helenium* 'Moerheim Beauty', creeping purple-leaved bugle (*Ajuga reptans* 'Catlin's Giant') and red-tinged Japanese blood grass (*Imperata cylindrica* 'Rubra').

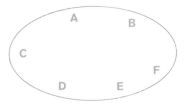

purple passion

You need

2 *Astelia nervosa*
  'Westland' **A**

2 *Osteospermum*
  'Nasinga Purple' **B**

A gorgeous mosaic-covered trough has inspired this planting of bronze astelias and deep purple osteospermums, a striking combination for a sunny spot.

Planting & care Plant the trough in late spring when all risk of frost has passed using a free-draining, moisture-retentive compost. Apply a liquid fertilizer every two weeks and remove the heads of the osteospermums as they fade to encourage more flowers to come.

Or you could try using green and white striped spider plants (*Chlorophytum comosum* 'Variegatum') instead of the bronze astelias, and *Osteospermum* 'Whirlygig', which has eye-catching white crimped flowers with blue backs to the petals.

seed-raised show

You need

1 *Helianthus annus* cultivar (dwarf sunflower) **A**

3 *Phlox* 'Bobby Sox' **B**

3 *Tagetes* 'Lemon Gem' **C**

This cheerful tubful of annuals has been raised from seed on a windowsill indoors, a cheap and satisfying way to fill the garden and offering a much wider choice of interesting and exciting plants to try.

Planting & care Sow the seeds in early spring in small pots of seed compost. Sprinkle the marigold and phlox seeds on the surface of the compost, then sieve a little extra compost over the top to cover lightly. The larger sunflower seeds can be poked individually into the compost about 2.5 cm (1 in) deep. Place upturned clear plastic bags over the pots and hold in place with elastic bands. Stand on a sunny windowsill and keep the compost just moist. When the seedlings are big enough to handle, pot them on into individual pots. Plant up the tub in late spring or early summer when all risk of frost has passed using a free-draining compost, and deadhead regularly to keep the flowers coming.

Or you could try buying the young plants rather than raising your own from seed.

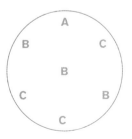

bright white

A dark glazed tub hosts a dazzling display of bright white flowers and foliage, an elegant summer show for sun or partial shade.

You need

1 *Argyranthemum* cultivar **A**

3 *Impatiens walleriana* Accent 'White' (busy Lizzie) **B**

2 *Lobelia erinus* cultivar **C**

1 *Hypoestes* cultivar (polka dot plant) **D**

Planting & care Plant the tub in late spring when all risk of frost has passed using a free-draining, moisture-retentive compost. Keep the compost just moist and feed every two weeks with a liquid fertilizer. Deadhead the busy Lizzies and argyranthemum regularly to encourage them to produce more blooms.

Or you could try using the same plants in shades of pastel pink. Try *Argyranthemum* 'Mary Wootton', busy Lizzie Accent 'Pink', pale pink lobelia and a pretty pink-spotted polka dot plant.

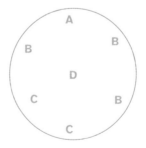

firework display

You need

2 *Pelargonium* 'Fireworks' **A**

1 *Heuchera* cultivar (coral flower) **B**

1 *Nemesia* cultivar **C**

A plain grey galvanized tub is the perfect foil for a metallic heuchera, lilac nemesia and pale pink pelargonium 'Fireworks' with exotic curled petals. The display will last all summer.

Planting & care Plant the tub in late spring when all risk of frost has passed using a free-draining compost. Apply a liquid feed every two weeks and deadhead regularly to encourage a succession of blooms. As the risk of frost approaches in the autumn, transfer the heuchera to the garden. If you want to save the pelargoniums for next year, pot them into individual pots of free-draining compost and keep on a sunny windowsill indoors. Cut back hard in the spring and use in next year's tubs.

Or you could try going for a softer look by replacing the dark, bold heuchera with light, frilly silver-leaved thyme (*Thymus vulgaris* 'Silver Posie') and using a white or soft pink nemesia.

```
A      A


B      C
```

scent of summer

You need

4 *Nicotiana* cultivar (tobacco plant) **A**

8 purple *Viola* (pansy) **B**

8 cream *Viola* (pansy) **C**

8 *Lobelia erinus* cultivar **D**

Beautiful tobacco plants, with their exotic, heady scent, make great subjects for tubs near the house. Here they are combined with dusky purple and cream pansies and lobelias, making a gorgeous display for a shady spot.

Planting & care Plant the tub in late spring when all risk of frost has passed using a moisture-retentive, free-draining compost. Be sure to choose scented tobacco plants (not all of them are) and neat edging lobelia rather than the trailing type. Remove the flowers as they fade to encourage the plants to produce more and apply a liquid feed every two weeks.

Or you could try heliotrope (*Heliotropium arborescens*), another scented plant with lovely purple flowers. Also known as cherry pie, the plant has an intoxicating sweet scent. Use in the tub instead of the tobacco plants and place in full sun.

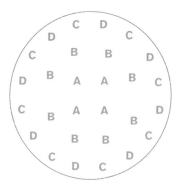

fantasy foliage

You need

2 *Pelargonium* cultivar
(fancy-leaved geranium) **A**

2 *Solenostemon* cultivar
(coleus) **B**

2 *Phormium tenax* cultivar
(New Zealand flax) **C**

1 *Chamaecyparis pisifera*
'Filifera' **D**

2 *Plectranthus forsteri*
'Marginatus' **E**

2 *Hypoestes* cultivar (polka
dot plant) **F**

2 *Iresine herbstii* cultivar **G**

2 *Helichrysum petiolare*
'Limelight' **H**

2 *Hedera helix* cultivar (ivy) **I**

A rich mixture of colours, this eye-catching windowbox proves that foliage can be just as colourful as flowers. The display features plants of a wide range of habits – spiky, bushy, trailing – with curls and stripes for added interest.

Planting & care Plant the box in late spring when all risk of frost has passed using a free-draining, moisture-retentive compost. Insert fertilizer spikes designed for foliage plants into the compost to do the feeding for you. Keep the compost moist: there are a lot of plants packed in here. At the end of the season, transfer the hardy phormium and chamaecyparis to the garden.

Or you could try a pink, purple and silver display with pink-leaved *Phormium* 'Dazzler', a purple-leaved coleus such as 'Palisandra', silver helichrysum and *Plectranthus argentatus*, and a pink and cream-leaved pelargonium, such as 'Miss Burdett Coutts'.

purple haze

You need

3 *Salvia farinacea* (mealy sage) **A**

8 *Petunia* cultivar **B**

6 *Isotoma axillaris* (laurentia) **C**

8 *Lobelia erinus* 'String of Pearls' **D**

A haze of purple flowers adorns a simple white bowl in a display reminiscent of a summer meadow. There is star-like laurentia, blousy petunias in dark and pale purple, lobelias around the edges and spikes of salvia in the centre.

Planting & care Plant the tub in late spring when all risk of frost has passed using a free-draining compost. Apply a liquid feed every two weeks and deadhead regularly to encourage the plants to produce further blooms.

Or you could try extending the meadow theme further and including some annual grasses, such as greater quaking grass (*Briza maxima*), which looks a little like oats, or hare's tail (*Lagurus ovatus*), which has soft, fluffy heads tinged with purple.

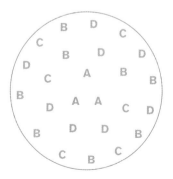

silver service

You need

2 *Dianthus* cultivar (pinks) **A**

2 *Euonymus fortunei*
cultivar (spindle) **B**

1 *Convolvulus cneorum* **C**

The soft, silvery leaves of this evergreen convolvulus make a fine foil for many other container plants. Here they are teamed with an evergreen spindle with cream and green foliage, and pretty pinks with mounds of silver foliage and scented pink flowers.

Planting & care Plant the container at any time of year using a free-draining compost and topdress with a layer of horticultural grit. Sprinkle a little bonemeal or other slow-release fertilizer into the top of the container each year in spring. Cut back the shrubs if necessary to keep tidy and remove the flowers from the pinks as they fade.

Or you could try a white and silver plant display using *Euonymus fortunei* 'Emerald Gaiety', which has green and white leaves, and a white-flowered pink, such as the old-fashioned 'Mrs Sinkins', 'Haytor White' or 'Musgrave's Pink', all of which have scented flowers.

shade lovers

You need

1 *Matteuccia struthiopteris* (shuttlecock fern) **A**

1 *Alchemilla mollis* (lady's mantle) **B**

1 *Tolmiea menziesii* 'Taff's Gold' (pick-a-back plant) **C**

1 *Hosta* cultivar **D**

Colours are clearer in the shade, and this study in green benefits from lower light levels where the subtleties of colour can be really appreciated. Lime greens and blue-greens mingle to create a gentle harmony.

Planting & care Plant the tub at any time of year using a moisture-retentive compost to which you have added some well-rotted manure or garden compost. Keep the compost moist at all times and fork a little bonemeal or other slow-release fertilizer into the top of the compost each spring. These plants are herbaceous and will die down over winter so remove the dead foliage in autumn or spring ready for the new spring growth.

Or you could try other shade-loving perennials, such as rodgersia with its large, rhubarb-like leaves, deadnettles (*Lamium*) with foliage in shades of silver, green or yellow, or barrenwort (*Epimedium*) with lovely heart-shaped mottled leaves on thin wiry stems.

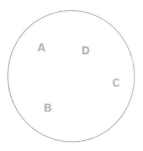

hanging gardens

You need

4 *Verbena* Tapien Series
'Purple' **A**

4 *Nemesia* Poetry
'Candyfloss' **B**

4 *Pelargonium* cultivar
(geranium) **C**

6 *Diascia* cultivar **D**

2 *Helichrysum petiolare*
'Limelight' **E**

2 *Brachyscome* cultivar
(Swan River daisy) **F**

6 *Lobelia* 'Waterfall Light
Lavender' **G**

This pretty hanging basket is a cascade of colour, overflowing with all the favourite summer basket plants. Pelargoniums, verbenas, Swan River daisies, diascias and nemesias mingle to create a glorious show.

Planting & care Plant the basket in late spring when all risk of frost has passed using a moisture-retentive compost to which you have added some moisture-retaining gel crystals. Insert some fertilizer spikes to take care of the feeding for you as there are a lot of plants in a small amount of compost, and they'll need a regular supply of nutrients to flower well. Deadhead regularly through summer to keep the flowers coming.

Or you could try sticking to soft pastel shades and replacing the purple verbena with 'Tapien White' or 'Pink Parfait', and using pale pink pelargoniums.

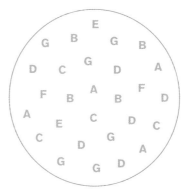

clematis creation

You need

1 *Clematis* 'Elsa Späth' **A**

1 *Clematis* 'Miss Bateman' **B**

1 *Clematis* 'Liberation' **C**

Gorgeous showy clematis, like these large-flowered cultivars, are ideal for container culture. The big, open blooms appear in early summer. Choose two or three cultivars that look good growing up together.

Planting & care Plant the tub at any time of year using a moisture-retentive compost. Plant the clematis with their crowns around 8 cm (3 in) below the surface of the compost to protect against clematis wilt and encourage further stems to develop. Add a wigwam to support them. Place in a sunny position with the tub in shade if possible as these plants like cool roots. Cut back each of the stems to a pair of strong healthy buds each year in early spring and fork a little bonemeal or other slow-release fertilizer into the top of the compost.

Or you could try some of the other large-flowered clematis, such as 'Nelly Moser', a much-loved favourite with pink flowers with a dark stripe down each petal, or 'Beauty of Worcester' with double blue flowers.

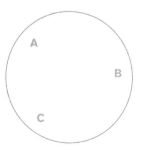

red, white and blue

You need

5 *Verbena* Flamenco 'Dark Red' **A**

5 *Lobelia erinus* 'Blue Star' **B**

5 *Calibrachoa* Celebration 'White' **C**

A basic plastic hanging pot has been filled with three summer beauties in contrasting colours — red verbena, blue lobelia and white calibrachoa — so full and healthy that the pot is no longer visible.

Planting & care Plant the hanging pot in late spring when all risk of frost has passed using a free-draining compost. Choose a pot with a built-in water reservoir if possible to cut down on watering. Apply a liquid fertilizer every two weeks and keep the compost just moist. Pick out the growing tips of the verbena and calibrachoa as they grow to encourage the plants to bush up.

Or you could try using blue daisies (*Felicia amelloides*) instead of the lobelia if you want a clearer blue. They are similar to Swan River daisies (*Brachyscome*), but the colour is pure blue.

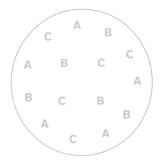

pansy perfection

You need

4 *Viola* cultivar (pansy;
2 purple, 2 orange) **A**

4 *Viola* cultivar
(smaller flowered viola;
2 purple, 2 yellow) **B**

3 *Argyranthemum* cultivar **C**

5 *Lobularia maritima*
(alyssum) **D**

4 *Hedera helix* cultivar (ivy) **E**

With all the other choices available, we often forget pansies for summer displays, yet they flower reliably right through the season. Here they are teamed up with white alyssum, ivy and argyranthemums in a windowbox.

Planting & care Plant the box in late spring when all risk of frost has passed using a moisture-retentive compost. Keep the compost just moist and apply a liquid fertilizer every two weeks to keep the flowers coming. Deadhead the argyranthemums, pansies and violas regularly.

Or you could try combining brighter plants with the colourful pansies for a more eye-catching display. Try some of the tender foliage plants on offer for summer containers, such as coleus (*Solenostemon*) in vivid shades of crimson, purple, orange and lime green, or the lovely purple-leaved Persian shield (*Strobilanthes dyeriana*).

soft summer pinks

This soft floriferous display of pastel pinks is the epitome of summer, with pelargoniums and fuchsias playing the leading role. Here the plants fill a windowbox, but they'd look just as good in a hanging basket or patio tub.

You need

4 *Pelargonium* cultivar (geranium) **A**

3 *Fuchsia* cultivar **B**

2 *Diascia* cultivar **C**

2 *Nemesia* cultivar **D**

2 *Impatiens* cultivar (busy Lizzie) **E**

2 *Petunia* 'Surfinia Rose Vein' **F**

2 *Verbena* 'Tapien White' **G**

2 *Sutera* cultivar (bacopa) **H**

1 *Glechoma hederacea* 'Variegata' **I**

Planting & care Plant the windowbox in late spring when all risk of frost has passed using a moisture-retentive compost to which you have added some moisture-retaining gel crystals. Keep the compost just moist and apply a liquid fertilizer every two weeks. Deadhead the plants regularly to maintain a good show of flowers.

Or you could try other soft pink summer flowers, such as osteospermum 'Arusha', pink lobelias, pale pink begonias, such as the double-flowered 'Pink Cloud', soft pink argyranthemums, such as 'Summit Pink' or the double-flowered 'Summersong Rose', or pale pink snapdragons (*Antirrhinum*).

a feast for the senses

You need

2 *Cosmos atrosanguineus*
(chocolate cosmos) **A**

2 *Solanum rantonnetii*
'Royal Robe' (blue potato
bush) **B**

2 *Pelargonium* 'Royal Oak'
(scented geranium) **C**

4 *Calibrachoa* cultivar **D**

This lovely collection of tender perennials is not just easy on the eye but on the nose too. Chocolate cosmos, with chocolate-scented flowers, sits alongside a pretty blue potato bush with a heady perfume and the spicy-scented pelargonium 'Royal Oak'.

Planting & care Plant the tub in late spring when all risk of frost has passed using a free-draining compost. The display is designed to be viewed from one side only, so the taller plants are arranged at the back. Keep the compost just moist and apply a liquid fertilizer every two weeks or so through the summer. Deadhead regularly to encourage a succession of flowers.

Or you could try a container with just scented pelargoniums of different types. 'Lady Plymouth' has pretty cream-edged leaves with a eucalyptus scent, 'Mabel Grey' has a strong lemon scent, while 'Graveolens' smells of roses. Position the container where you will brush past it and release the scent.

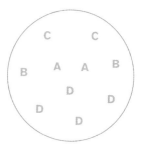

wierd and wonderful

You need

1 *Ricinus communis* (castor oil plant) **A**

3 *Amaranthus caudatus* cultivar (love lies bleeding; 2 red, 1 green) **B**

1 *Aeonium* 'Zwartkop' **C**

1 *Brassica* cultivar (ornamental brassica) **D**

2 *Petunia* 'Mirage Midnight' **E**

1 *Pelargonium* cultivar (geranium) **F**

1 *Tradescantia pallida* 'Purpurea' **G**

This unusual display of deep reds, purples and greens focuses on unusual foliage, with the large showy leaves of a castor oil plant, a curly grey-green brassica, purple-leaved tradescantia and black aeonium.

Planting & care Plant the container in late spring when all risk of frost has passed using a moisture-retentive compost. Keep the compost moist and apply a liquid feed every two weeks. Deadhead the flowers as they fade to keep them coming. As the risk of frost approaches later in the year, pot up the aeonium, pelargonium and tradescantia into small pots and enjoy them as houseplants on a sunny windowsill.

Or you could try the rich reds and purples of coleus (*Solenostemon*) instead of the amaranthus and brassica to add more colour.

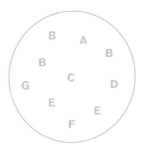

pink daisies

You need

1 *Pericallis* x *hybrida*
'Senetti Magenta Bi-colour'
(cineraria) **A**

1 *Pericallis* x *hybrida*
Senetti Series 'Magenta'
(cineraria) **B**

2 *Argyranthemum* 'Summer
Melody' **C**

A muted grey tub is the perfect foil for a dazzling array of pink daisy flowers. Brilliantly bright cinerarias and softer pink argyranthemums are a wonderful combination for early summer before most summer bedding plants have started flowering.

Planting & care Plant the tub in late spring when all risk of frost has passed. Although the cinerarias are fairly hardy, argyranthemums will be cut down by late frosts. Use a free-draining compost and keep it just moist. Apply a liquid feed every two weeks and deadhead regularly to maintain a succession of flowers.

Or you could try deep blue and white cineraria 'Senetti Bi-colour Blue' with a white argyranthemum, such as 'Summersong White' or 'Ping-Pong'.

```
B        A


C        C
```

warm welcome

You need

1 *Argyranthemum* 'Jamaica Primrose' **A**

2 *Phygelius* cultivar (Cape figwort) **B**

2 *Molinia caerulea* subsp. *caerulea* 'Variegata' (variegated purple moor grass) **C**

2 *Ophiopogon planiscapus* 'Nigrescens' **D**

2 *Calibrachoa* cultivar **E**

4 *Peperomia* cultivar **F**

6 *Hedera helix* cultivar (ivy) **G**

A lovely combination of grasses and flowers in rich shades of russet and yellow offers a warm welcome on the doorstep. The colour scheme has been designed to tie in with the yellow sandstone wall behind.

Planting & care Plant the tub in late spring when all risk of frost has passed using a free-draining compost. Keep the compost just moist and apply a liquid fertilizer every two weeks. Deadhead regularly to encourage more flowers to come.

Or you could try lightening the display, using a pale yellow phygelius, such as Candydrops Series 'Cream', and swapping the black ophiopogon and peperomia for Bowles's golden sedge (*Carex elata* 'Aurea') and a pale heuchera, such as 'Key Lime Pie'.

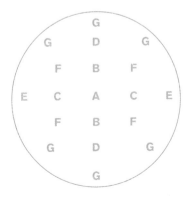

box of blooms

You need

3 *Pelargonium* Trend 'Lavender' **A**

2 *Petunia* 'Surfinia Purple Vein' **B**

2 *Brachyscome* cultivar (Swan River daisy) **C**

This windowbox, adorning a balcony rail, is packed with blooms, with geraniums, petunias and Swan River daisies flowering their socks off. Feed and deadhead regularly to achieve such a magnificent display.

Planting & care Plant the box in late spring when all risk of frost has passed using a moisture-retentive compost. Pick out the growing tips of the plants when they are young to encourage bushiness: this will delay flowering a little but increase the number of flowers produced. Feed every week with a liquid fertilizer and remove blooms as soon as they fade to encourage more to be produced. Keep the compost just moist at all times.

Or you could try the same display in white, with pure white pelargonium 'Aphrodite', *Petunia* 'Surfinia Vanilla' and white Swan River daisies.

precious gems

You need

4 *Verbena* Romance 'Purple' **A**

4 *Begonia semperflorens* cultivar **B**

2 *Helichrysum petiolare* **C**

An elegant square silver planter has been filled with verbenas, begonias and silver helichysums arranged like gems in a jewellery box. Place on a dining table outdoors or on the top of a wall where it can be appreciated at close quarters.

Planting & care Plant the container in late spring when all risk of frost has passed using a moisture-retentive compost. Tuck a little dried Spanish moss around the plants to hide the compost. Pick out the growing tips of the plants when they are young to encourage bushiness. Water and feed regularly and trim off any stray stems to keep the plants neat.

Or you could try rich ruby-red begonias, which have a jewel-like quality, with scarlet or deep pink verbena. Be sure to choose a low-growing, compact verbena cultivar such as Romance 'Pink' or 'Red'.

sweet scent

You need

10 *Lathyrus odoratus* 'Galaxy Mixed' (sweet pea) **A**

4 *Pelargonium* 'Flower Fairy Berry' (geranium) **B**

6 *Petunia* 'Purple Lady' **C**

6 *Pelargonium* (scented-leaved geranium) **D**

A wigwam of hazel twigs supports pretty scented sweet peas in mixed colours, underplanted with pink petunias and pelargoniums, and a selection of scented-leaved pelargoniums.

Planting & care Plant the tub in late spring when all risk of frost has passed. Sweet peas do best in a rich compost, so mix plenty of well-rotted manure or garden compost into the bottom of the tub as you fill it with moisture-retentive compost. Apply a liquid fertilizer every two weeks and deadhead all the plants regularly to maintain a succession of flowers.

Or you could try the everlasting pea (*Lathyrus latifolius*), which is a hardy perennial climber. It comes up every year with pretty blue-green foliage and rich pink flowers so it can stay in the tub permanently.

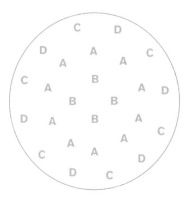

mini meadow

You need

4 *Jasione laevis* (sheep's bit) **A**

2 *Scabiosa* 'Pink Mist' (small scabious) **B**

4 *Deschampsia flexuosa* 'Tatra Gold' (wavy hair grass) **C**

2 *Festuca glauca* 'Blaufuchs' (blue fescue) **D**

A tin bath has been planted with a rather glamorous version of a wildflower meadow. The pretty pink and lilac nodding heads of sheep's bit and small scabious are surrounded by designer grasses in blue and green.

Planting & care Plant the bath at any time of year using a free-draining compost. First make sure there are plenty of drainage holes in the bottom of the bath – if not, make some with a drill. Keep the compost just moist and fork a little bonemeal or other slow-release fertilizer into the top of the compost each spring.

Or you could try including diminutive alpine poppies (*Papaver alpinum*) in the bath to extend the meadow theme. These sweet little perennials come in pretty shades of white, pink, yellow and orange and should self-sow to produce different colours each year.

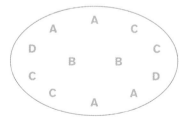

regal roses

You need

4 *Rosa* 'Ruby Anniversary'
(rose) **A**

A handsome Versailles planter, coloured with scarlet woodstain, is home to a group of rich red patio rose 'Ruby Anniversary'. If deadheaded, the roses will provide many weeks of vivid colour throughout summer.

Planting & care Plant the roses at any time of year in a moisture-retentive, free-draining compost to which you have added some well-rotted manure or garden compost. Fork a little bonemeal or other slow-release fertilizer into the top of the compost each spring and mulch with well-rotted manure or garden compost. Prune the roses in late autumn.

Or you could try staining a wooden planter with lilac or blue woodstain and planting with the floribunda (cluster-flowered) rose 'Shocking Blue', which has pretty fragrant lilac-purple flowers.

A   A

A   A

perfumed perfection

You need

3 *Matthiola incana* (stocks) **A**

5 *Viola* cultivar (smaller flowered viola) **B**

Pure white stocks and soft mauve violas in a galvanized container make an effective display against the rich blue background of the shed behind. The stocks have a wonderful perfume, so place the tub on a table close to nose level.

Planting & care Plant the tub in late spring when all risk of frost has passed using a free-draining, moisture-retentive compost. Feed every two weeks with a liquid fertilizer and deadhead the flowers regularly to prolong the display.

Or you could try using night-scented stocks (*Matthiola longipetala* subsp. *bicornis*), which have smaller flowers in white and shades of pink or mauve but the most magnificent perfume in the evenings. Place the container on the table on the patio for those warm summer evenings under the stars.

snappy show

You need

2 *Antirrhinum majus* 'Bells Red' (trumpet-flowered snapdragon) **A**

2 *Antirrhinum majus* Tahiti 'Pink and White' (snapdragon) **B**

4 *Solenostemon* 'Wizard' (coleus) **C**

2 *Hedera helix* cultivar (ivy) **D**

Cheerful snapdragons fill a rustic timber planter with vibrant chocolate and lime coleus and ivies to soften the edges. Choose a range of snapdragons with different flower shapes, including trumpet-flowered, azalea-flowered and traditional snaps.

Planting & care Plant the container in late spring when all risk of frost has passed using a moisture-retentive compost. Keep the compost just moist and feed every two weeks with a liquid fertilizer. Deadhead the snapdragons regularly to prolong the flowering period.

Or you could try snapdragon 'Black Prince' with the chocolate and lime coleus. The foliage is bronze and the flowers are a wonderful velvety dark red. Team up with lime green *Helichrysum petiolare* 'Limelight' around the edges of the tub instead of the ivy.

dainty daisies

You need

1 *Felicia amelloides* (blue daisy) **A**

2 *Brachyscome* cultivar (Swan River daisy) **B**

A handsome ceramic wall pot is home to a simple combination of daisies, both Swan River daisies in lilac and blue daisies in clear blue, forming a soft mound of fine foliage topped with a profusion of dainty flowers.

Planting & care Plant the pot in late spring when all risk of frost has passed using a moisture-retentive compost. Because the pot doesn't hold much compost and will dry out quickly, add some moisture-retaining gel crystals to the compost. Water daily and feed every two weeks with a liquid fertilizer. Deadhead regularly to maintain a succession of flowers.

Or you could try combining the variegated blue daisy (*Felicia amoena* 'Variegata') with its bright cream-edged foliage, with a white Swan River daisy, such as *Brachyscome* 'White Splendour'.

purple fountain

You need

1 *Pennisetum setaceum* 'Rubrum' (fountain grass) **A**

4 *Scaevola aemula* (fan flower) **B**

A gorgeous purple fountain grass makes a graceful centrepiece for a white wooden planter. It is surrounded by blue fan flowers for a pleasing contrast of colour and form.

Planting & care Plant the tub in late spring when all risk of frost has passed using a moisture-retentive compost. Keep the compost moist and apply a liquid fertilizer every two weeks. The fountain grass is perennial but not quite hardy, but you may get it to survive in the tub over winter by cutting off all the foliage in late autumn and wrapping the container in bubblewrap to protect it from frost. Unwrap in mid-spring and keep your fingers crossed for emerging foliage soon afterwards.

Or you could try one of the pink pennisetums, such as *Pennisetum glaucum* 'Jester' with rich pink, burgundy and bronze tones to its foliage. Team up with deep pink Surfinia petunias for a colourful show.

```
B          B

     A

B          B
```

fancy fuchsias

You need

3 *Fuchsia* 'Garden News' **A**

4 *Verbena* 'Sissinghurst' **B**

2 *Scaevola aemula* (fan flower) **C**

Blousy pink fuchsias, deep pink verbena and rich blue fan flowers mingle together in a lovely aged terracotta bowl. The bowl, with its strong lines, lends itself to a soft and full planting with trailing stems and lots of flowers.

Planting & care Plant the bowl in late spring when all risk of frost has passed using a moisture-retentive compost. This bowl will dry out quickly, so it is a good idea to line it with plastic to retain moisture. Be sure to make some holes in the plastic in the bottom of the bowl. Water regularly and feed every two weeks with a liquid fertilizer. Remove the blooms as they fade to encourage more to come. This fuchsia is hardy so it can be transferred to the garden in the autumn.

Or you could try some of the other lovely fuchsias on offer, such as the unusually coloured 'Amazing Maisie' with pink and orange flowers, teamed up with pink and orange *Lantana camara* around the edges of the bowl.

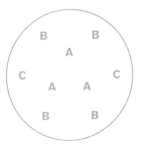

exotic beauties

A full and varied display of foliage and flowers is given an exotic feel by the dark, dusky leaves of fuchsia 'Thalia' and the strange black flowers of an unusual tender salvia.

You need

2 *Fuchsia* 'Thalia' **A**

3 *Bidens ferulifolia* **B**

3 *Pelargonium* cultivar
(ivy-leaved pelargonium) **C**

2 *Lotus berthelotii* **D**

1 *Tropaeolum* cultivar
(nasturtium) **E**

1 *Salvia discolor* **F**

Planting & care Be sure to choose a tall pot to allow the trailing plants plenty of space to trail. Plant the container in late spring when all risk of frost has passed using a moisture-retentive compost. Feed every two weeks with a liquid fertilizer and keep deadheading to maintain the display right through summer. The lotus will go on to produce bright red, claw-shaped flowers on its grey ferny foliage.

Or you could try leaving out the yellow bidens and replacing it with vivid scarlet Lantana camara instead for an even more dramatic effect.

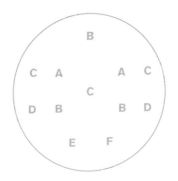

little gem

You need

1 *Lobelia erinus* cultivar **A**

A dainty wicker basket on a simple metal chain has been planted with a single sapphire-blue lobelia. Usually used as a filler, lobelia can hold its own as the star attraction.

Planting & care Plant the basket in late spring when all risk of frost has passed. First line the basket with plastic to retain moisture and hold the compost in place, then make a few drainage holes in the plastic to allow excess water to drain away. Fill the basket with moisture-retentive compost to which you have added some moisture-retaining gel crystals. Feed every two weeks with a liquid fertilizer to prolong the flowering period and water regularly to keep the compost moist.

Or you could try filling a number of identical baskets with lobelias in different shades of blue. Hang the baskets from a pergola over a seating area or from the branches of a tree close to the patio.

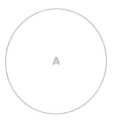

dizzy daisies

You need

1 *Lasthenia glabrata* **A**

3 *Calendula officinalis*
  (pot marigold) **B**

5 *Viola* cultivar (pansy) **C**

3 *Bellis perennis*
  cultivar (bellis daisy) **D**

A white wooden planter has been filled with
pansies and daisy flowers. A profusion of yellow
lasthenia flowers rises above the chunky blooms
of white bellis daisies and yellow pot marigolds.
Deep red pansies add a richer contrast of colour.

Planting & care Plant the tub in late spring when
all risk of frost has passed using a free-draining
compost. Feed every two weeks with a liquid fertilizer
and deadhead regularly to maintain a show of flowers.
Although the lasthenia is an annual, cut it back when
it becomes leggy and produces fewer flowers, and it
should grow again to produce a second flush of blooms.

Or you could try *Bidens ferulifolia* for a similar
effect if you can't find *Lasthenia glabrata*. The foliage
has a softer, more ferny appearance but the flowers
are a close match.

dark and mysterious

You need

2 *Lagurus ovatus*
(hare's tail) **A**

3 *Begonia rex* cultivar **B**

2 *Tradescantia zebrina*
(wandering jew) **C**

2 *Viola* 'Blackjack' (pansy) **D**

Sumptuous fancy-leaved begonias in shades of black, grey and pink are offset by grey-striped tradescantia, the fluffy heads of hare's tail and jet-black pansies, an eye-catching show for a shady spot in summer.

Planting & care Plant the trough in late spring when all risk of frost has passed using a moisture-retentive compost. Keep the compost just moist and feed from time to time with a liquid fertilizer. Remove the flowers from the pansies as they fade to encourage more blooms. At the end of the season as the risk of frost approaches, pot the begonias and tradescantias into individual pots and bring indoors as houseplants. Discard the annual hare's tail and pansies.

Or you could try other black flowers, such as fuchsia 'Roesse Blacky', pelargonium 'Black Rose', the black lily 'Landini' or the black arum *Zantedeschia* 'Black Forest' with its sinister cone-shaped flowers.

A	B	B	A
C		B		C
	D		D	

essence of summer

You need

1 *Argyranthemum* cultivar **A**

1 *Verbena* Tapien Pink **B**

6 *Pelargonium* 'Belle Ville Mixed' (geranium) **C**

2 *Helichrysum petiolare* **D**

1 *Fuchsia* cultivar **E**

A pretty blue-leaved argyranthemum forms a cloud of fine foliage and white flowers in a white wooden planter. It is underplanted with bright pink trailing geraniums, verbena, soft pink fuchsias and silver helichrysum, the essence of summer containers.

Planting & care Plant the tub in late spring when all risk of frost is past using a free-draining compost. Pick out the growing tips of the plants when small to encourage bushiness, and keep the compost just moist. Apply a liquid fertilizer every two weeks and deadhead all the plants regularly to maintain a show of flowers all season long.

Or you could try a pure white display with verbena Tapien 'White', pelargonium 'Belle Ville White' and the lovely hardy fuchsia 'Hawkshead'.

autumn beauties

cool cabbages

You need

3 ornamental cabbages **A**

3 *Viola* cultivar (pansy) **B**

2 *Euonymus fortunei* 'Emerald Gaiety' **C**

2 *Calluna vulgaris* cultivar (Scots heather) **D**

This cool autumn scheme of greens and whites features the frilly heads of ornamental cabbages with pansies, heathers and the striking foliage of euonymus in a simple terracotta bowl.

Planting & care Plant the tub in late summer using a moisture-retentive compost. Keep moist and remove the pansy flowers as they fade to encourage more to appear. When the cabbages and pansies are past their best, discard them and replace with fresh pansies and cabbages to extend the display through to spring.

Or you could try pink ornamental cabbages with pink heathers and pale pink or white pansies.

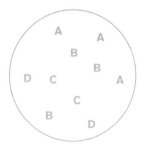

rich autumn pinks

You need

3 *Calluna vulgaris* cultivar (Scots heather; 2 white, 1 pink) **A**

3 *Viola* cultivar (pansy) **B**

A simple collection of heathers and pansies in white and rich pink fills a woven twig wall basket in autumn. The colour scheme has been chosen to complement the blue-stained shed on which the basket is hanging.

Planting & care Plant the basket in late summer using a moisture-retentive ericaceous (acidic) compost. Arrange two white heathers at the back of the basket, one on either side, and the pink heather in front and between the two. Pop the pansies along the front of the basket, firm and water well. Water regularly, especially if the basket is hanging in a warm, sunny position. When the plants finish flowering, discard the pansies and plant the heathers out in the garden.

Or you could try using autumn-flowering gentians (*Gentiana sino-ornata*) instead of the pansies. They have vivid blue trumpet flowers (perfect with a blue background) and mossy green foliage. They are perennial plants so transfer them to the garden when they finish flowering. Team them with white heathers.

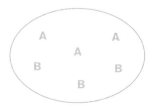

vegetable basket

You need

4 ornamental cabbages **A**

6 *Calluna vulgaris*
   cultivar (Scots heather) **B**

3 *Hedera helix* cultivar (ivy) **C**

A simple wire hanging basket has been lined with conifer foliage and filled with pretty pink cabbages, heathers and ivies for a soft and appealing autumn display.

Planting & care Plant the basket in late summer. Start by lining the empty basket with conifer foliage to hold the compost in place. The foliage will gradually turn an attractive russet brown. Fill the basket with moisture-retentive ericaceous (acidic) compost and arrange the plants in the top. Plant the central cabbage a little higher than the others to make it more visible. Keep the compost moist, especially if the basket is hanging in a warm, sunny position. When the plants have finished flowering, discard the cabbages and plant the heathers in the garden. The ivies can be kept in the basket for a winter display.

Or you could try replacing the cabbages with pale pink osteospermums, with their big, bold daisy flowers. They start flowering in late spring or early summer, but will still be going strong in autumn.

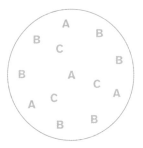

fiery glow

You need

1 *Physalis alkekengi* (Chinese lantern) **A**

2 orange chrysanthemums **B**

1 *Lysimachia nummularia* (creeping Jenny) **C**

1 *Ajania pacifica* 'Desert Flame' **D**

1 *Carex oshimensis* 'Evergold' (sedge) **E**

1 *Sedum* 'Lemon Ball' (stonecrop) **F**

This stunning display of Chinese lanterns and bright orange chrysanthemums fills a windowbox with fiery autumn colours. The windowbox has been painted pale yellow to set off the colour of the plants magnificently.

Planting & care Plant the windowbox in late summer using a moisture-retentive compost. Choose bushy chrysanthemum plants with plenty of buds. Place the display in a sheltered spot and keep the compost just moist. Remove the chrysanthemum flowers as they fade. Although all the plants are perennials, this is only a temporary display as there are too many plants in such a small space. Transfer the plants to the garden after flowering and replace with a winter-interest display.

Or you could try bright yellow chrysanthemums for an all-gold display. Use three chrysanthemum plants and leave out the Chinese lanterns.

winter winners

winter wonders

You need

5 *Cyclamen* **A**

6 *Viola* cultivar (purple
   bedding violas) **B**

A colourful windowbox can brighten up even the dullest of winter days. Cheerful cyclamen in red, pink and white are underplanted with purple violas in a pretty late-winter display for a sheltered spot.

Planting & care Plant the windowbox in early to midwinter using a free-draining container compost. Make sure the cyclamen are hardy plants that have been bred to grow outside, as some are raised for indoor use. Place the windowbox in a sheltered spot where it will be protected from the worst of the winter wet. Water sparingly to keep the compost just moist. Discard the plants when they have finished flowering in spring.

Or you could try a more formal mixture of all-red cyclamen and white violas. Add some variegated ivy to trail over the front of the box.

advanced guard

You need

20 early-flowering species crocus bulbs, such as *Crocus ancyrensis* or *C. reticulatus* **A**

15 *Iris reticulata* bulbs **B**

The warmth of the wall on which this terracotta pot is fixed will advance the flowering period of these sweet little crocuses and irises and bring them into flower in late winter – a little taste of the spring to come.

Planting & care Plant up the pot in autumn using a free-draining compost. Fill to within 8 cm (3 in) of the rim of the pot and arrange the bulbs on top of the compost, pointed ends uppermost. Add another 5 cm (2 in) of compost and firm lightly. Hang the pot on a sunny, sheltered wall and keep the compost just moist over winter. Feed with a liquid fertilizer after the bulbs have finished flowering, or plant them out in the garden instead and use the pot for summer bedding.

Or you could try growing snowdrops (*Galanthus*) and winter aconites (*Eranthis*) in the pot, both of which naturally flower in late winter, for a cheerful yellow and white display.

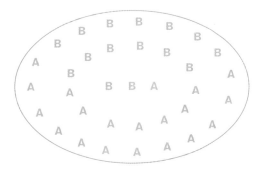

greens and creams

You need

1 *Hebe* 'Silver Queen' **A**

3 *Carex conica* 'Snowline' (sedge) **B**

3 *Carex pilulifera* 'Tinney's Princess' (sedge) **C**

6 *Hedera helix* cultivar (ivy) **D**

This pleasingly curvy terracotta pot contains a selection of evergreen foliage in shades of cream and green: pretty variegated ivies, stripy sedges and a bushy hebe in the centre, which will produce lovely pinky-purple flowers from mid- to late summer.

Planting & care Plant the tub at any time of year using a free-draining container compost. Keep the compost moist and fork a little bonemeal or other slow-release fertilizer into the top of the compost each year in spring. Remove the hebe flowers as they fade and trim the ivies if they become straggly.

Or you could try growing *Hebe* 'Autumn Glory', which has bronze shoots, red-edged leaves and lovely purple-blue flowers from midsummer right through autumn. Combine it with one of the brown-leaved sedges, such as *Carex petriei* or *C. comans*.

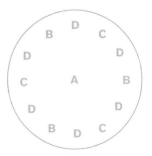

precious metals

You need

1 *Phormium tenax* 'Bronze' (New Zealand flax) **A**

1 *Heuchera* 'Pewter Moon' (coral flower) **B**

1 *Erica carnea* cultivar (winter heath) **C**

This stylish metallic tub contains spiky bronze New Zealand flax and pewter-leaved coral flower, with rich pink heather to brighten the scheme – a handsome and sophisticated display for the dull winter months.

Planting & care Plant the tub at any time of year using a free-draining compost. Keep the compost moist and fork a little bonemeal or other slow-release fertilizer into the top of the compost each year in spring. All the plants are evergreen, so the container will look good all year round, although the scheme will come to life when the heather blooms in winter.

Or you could try growing the plants in a galvanized metal container, such as a dustbin, trough or large bucket. Don't forget to make plenty of drainage holes in the bottom of the container if it hasn't been designed with plants in mind.

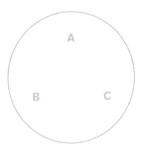

evergreen elegance

You need

1 *Viburnum tinus* (laurustinus) **A**

2 *Skimmia japonica* cultivar **B**

2 *Gaultheria procumbens* (checkerberry) **C**

2 *Heuchera* cultivar (coral flower) **D**

10 *Hedera helix* cultivar (ivy) **E**

This windowbox is overflowing with handsome evergreen foliage, elegant winter flowers and berries. The lovely scented laurustinus flowers will be replaced by black berries as the season progresses, while the smart red skimmia buds will open into full white blooms.

Planting & care Plant the windowbox in autumn using a moisture-retentive compost. Keep the compost moist by regular watering if the box is sheltered from the rain. Fork a little bonemeal or other slow-release fertilizer into the top of the compost each year in spring.

Or you could try creating a formal green and white display using gorgeously scented white-flowered Christmas box (*Sarcococca confusa*) instead of the skimmias and *Gaultheria mucronata* 'Wintertime' with bright white berries. Replace the bronze-leaved coral flower with *Heuchera* 'Snow Storm', which has green leaves with white marbling.

jolly jumble

You need

1 *Erica carnea* cultivar (winter heath) **A**

2 *Juniperus* cultivar (juniper) **B**

2 *Senecio cineraria* (cineraria) **C**

2 *Vinca major* 'Variegata' (periwinkle) **D**

4 *Cyclamen* **E**

1 *Solanum pseudocapsicum* (winter cherry) **F**

1 *Viola* cultivar (pansy) **G**

3 *Hedera helix* cultivar (ivy) **H**

A plain terracotta tub has been planted with a jumble of foliage, fruits and flowers for late winter. This cheerful display features a wide range of colours, textures and forms and needs to be placed in a sheltered position.

Planting & care Plant the tub in autumn using a free-draining compost. The display is designed to be viewed from one side only, so the taller plants are arranged at the back and the shorter plants at the front. Stand the tub in front of a wall, hedge or fence in a sunny spot sheltered from wind, rain and frosts.

Or you could try creating a similar display with tougher plants that can withstand colder weather. Leave out the cineraria, cyclamen and winter cherry and replace them with silvery *Artemisia arborescens* (wormwood), *Gaultheria mucronata* 'Cherry Ripe', with its red berries, and pale pink pansies.

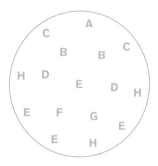

frosted berries

You need

1 *Skimmia japonica* subsp.
   reevesiana **A**

3 *Euonymus fortunei*
   'Emerald 'n' Gold'
   (spindle) **B**

3 *Hedera helix* cultivar (ivy) **C**

6 *Tiarella cordifolia* (foam
   flower) **D**

The plentiful red berries of skimmia look especially lovely when dusted with frost. Here they are combined with golden spindle, variegated ivy and tiarella in a terracotta-look resin tub, making a colourful and vibrant display for a shady spot in the dull winter months.

Planting & care Plant the container at any time of year using a free-draining, moisture-retentive compost. Stand in a shady position and keep the compost just moist. Fork a little bonemeal or other slow-release fertilizer into the top of the compost each spring. The skimmia will produce fragrant white flowers in spring, while the tiarella throws up tall stems of foamy white flowers in summer.

Or you could try a cool, all-white display using *Skimmia japonica* 'Fructo Albo' with its green spring flowers and pretty white berries.

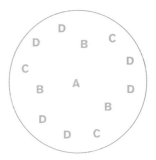

green tapestry

You need

1 *Skimmia* x *confusa* 'Kew Green' **A**

1 *Acorus gramineus* 'Ogon' (Japanese rush) **B**

1 *Leucothoe fontanesiana* 'Rainbow' **C**

1 *Lonicera nitida* 'Lemon Beauty' **D**

Four evergreen plants make an intricate tapestry with just their varied foliage to complete the picture: spiky stripy rush, mottled leucothoe, the tiny cream-edged leaves of lonicera and bold dark green skimmia, with the added bonus of its green flower buds.

Planting & care Plant the tub at any time of year using a free-draining, moisture-retentive ericaceous (acidic) compost. Fork a little bonemeal or other slow-release fertilizer into the compost in spring each year. The leucothoe will reward you with bell-shaped white flowers in spring, while the green buds of the skimmia will open to wonderfully fragrant white flowers.

Or you could try using other evergreen shrubs with interesting foliage, such as *Euonymus fortunei* cultivars, variegated or grey-leaved hebes, silvery *Convolvulus cneorum* or wormwood (*Artemisia*), or some of the yellow-splashed elaeagnus cultivars, such as *Elaeagnus* x *ebbingei* 'Limelight'.

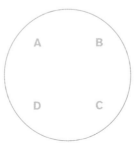

bare branches

You need

2 *Cornus sericea* 'Cardinal' (dogwood) **A**

3 *Erica carnea* 'Winter Snow' (winter heath) **B**

With their architectural branches in shades of red, orange and yellow, dogwoods are great for winter containers. Here the pinky stems of 'Cardinal' rise above a sea of white heather.

Planting & care Plant the container at any time of year using a free-draining ericaceous (acidic) compost. Fork a little bonemeal or other slow-release fertilizer into the top of the compost each spring. To maintain a display of coloured bare wood each winter, cut back all the stems hard to within two or three buds of the base in early spring. New stems will grow up through the spring and summer, ready to take on a lovely pinky hue in winter. Place in full sun for the best colour.

Or you could try a different colour scheme: perhaps lovely yellow-stemmed dogwood (*Cornus sericea* 'Flaviramea') with *Erica carnea* 'Golden Starlet' with lime green foliage and white flowers; or brilliant red-stemmed *C. alba* 'Sibirica' with *E. c.* 'Myretoun Ruby' or 'December Red', both of which have deep pink-red flowers.

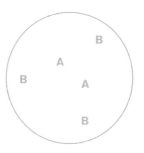

winter sunshine

You need

3 *Cyclamen* **A**

2 *Euonymus fortunei*
'Emerald 'n' Gold'
(spindle) **B**

1 ornamental chilli **C**

1 yellow *Solanum
pseudocapsicum* (winter
cherry) **D**

3 *Hedera helix* cultivar (ivy) **E**

A black windowbox is adorned with blousy white cyclamen, golden ornamental chillies, handsome variegated foliage and round winter cherry berries, soon to turn bright yellow themselves.

Planting & care Plant the box in autumn using a free-draining compost. Stand it in a sheltered position protected from winter winds, rain and frost: this is perfect for a sunny urban windowsill. Keep the compost just moist and apply a liquid fertilizer about two months after planting. When the plants have finished their display, discard the cyclamen, chilli and winter cherry but leave the spindles and ivy in the box to act as a framework for a spring display.

Or you could try a scarlet scheme with bright red cyclamen, a red chilli and a red winter cherry. Choose white and green ivies and *Euonymus fortunei* 'Emerald Gaiety' with its handsome white and green foliage.

	B		B	
A		A		A
	C		D	
E		E		E

all year round

evergreen collection

You need

1 *Acorus gramineus* 'Ogon' (Japanese rush) **A**

1 dwarf *Juniperus* cultivar (juniper) **B**

1 *Pittosporum tenuifolium* cultivar **C**

2 *Hedera helix* cultivar (ivy) **D**

This handsome collection of evergreen plants offers great variety in foliage colour, shape and habit, from trailing ivies to upright rushes, and from glossy pittosporum to fuzzy juniper.

Planting & care Plant the container at any time of year using a free-draining, moisture-retentive compost. Fork a little bonemeal or other slow-release fertilizer into the top of the compost each spring. Trim over the plants from time to time to remove any dead foliage and keep them tidy. The pittosporum will reward you with honey-scented, bell-shaped flowers in late spring. Although the pittosporum is basically hardy, it will do best in a sheltered site protected from hard frosts.

Or you could try growing these plants in a windowbox. Arrange two pittosporums and three junipers along the back of the box, evenly spaced, plant a Japanese rush at each end and arrange six trailing ivies along the front.

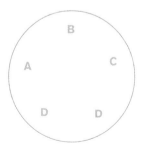

graceful grasses

You need

3 *Festuca* cultivars (fescue) **A**

A simple line of three grasses is the perfect foil for an elegant gold-rimmed trough. The soft sage green of the trough is picked up in the green grass foliage, a lovely harmonious centrepiece for an alfresco dining table.

Planting & care Plant the trough at any time of year using a free-draining compost to which you have added some moisture-retaining gel crystals. Space the grasses evenly in the trough: symmetry is vital here. Firm the compost and add a top-dressing of gravel, stone chips, horticultural grit or coloured ground glass mulch to cover the compost and add to the decorative appeal.

Or you could try painting a terracotta trough with soft blue acrylic paint instead and adding a silver rim using acrylic paint. Plant the painted trough with blue- or silver-leaved fescues, such as *Festuca glauca* 'Blaufuchs' or *F. valesiaca* 'Silbersee'.

tender succulents

You need

12 *Echeveria elegans* **A**

6 *Soleirolia soleirolii* (helxine) **B**

1 *Aeonium* 'Zwartkop' **C**

Rosette-forming succulents are perfect for hanging baskets as they clothe the sides with handsome fleshy foliage. Here pretty blue echeveria is teamed with black aeonium and underplanted with green helxine to cover the basket as the echeverias grow.

Planting & care Plant the basket at any time of year using a free-draining compost. Space the helxine and echeverias evenly around the sides of the basket and plant the aeonium in the top. Hang the basket in a sunny, sheltered spot outside, but protect from cold weather in winter. These plants are tender and need to be kept above 10°C (50°F): a greenhouse or near a south-facing window indoors would be ideal.

Or you could try a similar effect using hardy houseleeks (*Sempervivum*), which can stay outside all year round. Choose a selection of different colours for a tapestry effect.

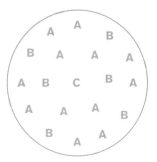

foliage and form

You need

1 *Hypericum* 'Magical Gold' **A**

1 *Acorus gramineus* 'Ogon' (Japanese rush) **B**

1 *Heuchera* 'Key Lime Pie' (coral flower) **C**

1 *Viola* cultivar (pansy) **D**

1 *Euonymus japonicus* 'Extase' (Japanese spindle) **E**

A square terracotta tub has been filled with a varied group of plants with interesting form and foliage in shades of greens and creams. The hypericum has aromatic foliage and produces fluffy yellow flowers in summer, followed by cream-coloured berries.

Planting & care Plant the tub at any time of year using a moisture-retentive compost. Fork a little bonemeal or other slow-release fertilizer into the top of the compost in spring each year. As the pansy becomes too leggy and finishes flowering, replace it with a fresh plant. This is likely to be two or three times a year.

Or you could try a study in greens and whites with *Euonymus japonicus* 'Albomarginatus', a white pansy, *Heuchera* 'Schneewittchen' with green leaves and white flowers, *Acorus gramineus* var *pusillus* with dark green leaves, and the white- and green-leaved dogwood *Cornus alba* 'Elegantissima'.

```
A          B


E     D    C
```

bold bamboo

You need

1 *Pleioblastus* cultivar (dwarf bamboo) **A**

4 x *Heucherella* cultivar **B**

This Japanese-style garden features a dwarf bamboo in a handsome black glazed tub. The rim of the tub is softened by the jagged foliage of heucherella in a pleasing contrast with the bamboo. A perfect year-round display for sun or partial shade.

Planting & care Plant the tub at any time of year using a moisture-retentive compost. Stand in sun or partial shade and fork a little bonemeal or other slow-release fertilizer into the top of the compost each year in spring. To keep the display neat and architectural, remove the tall spikes of heucherella flowers when they appear in early summer.

Or you could try black bamboo (*Phyllostachys nigra*) with its glossy black canes, teamed up with a purple- or pewter-leaved heuchera cultivar, such as *H. villosa* 'Palace Purple' or *H.* 'Pewter Moon'.

```
B              B

        A

B              B
```

romantic topiary

You need

1 *Buxus microphylla* (small-leaved box) **A**

Topiary usually adds a formal note to a garden or patio area, but this pretty box heart is a little more relaxed in its approach. Buy a ready-trained plant for instant effect, or train one yourself if you have the patience.

Planting & care Keep the topiary on its own in a pot of free-draining compost to maintain its foliage right down to compost level. Add a top-dressing of grit to smarten the appearance and suppress weeds. The plant stems have to be trained on a rigid wire heart to form such a perfect shape. If you are training your own topiary, loosely bind the long new shoots to the frame and trim off any other shoots that point in the wrong direction. To maintain a ready-trained topiary, simply keep the plant neat by trimming off new growths as they appear. Fork a little bonemeal or other slow-release fertilizer into the top of the compost each spring and keep the compost just moist.

Or you could try other topiary shapes, such as simple cones or balls, or a series of clipped tiers with bare stems in between. If you train your own, your imagination is the only limiting factor.

heavenly hostas

You need

1 *Picea pungens* 'Globosa'
(Colorado spruce) **A**

1 *Euonymus japonicus*
'Ovatus Aureus' (Japanese
spindle) **B**

1 *Hosta* 'Wide Brim' **C**

Hostas make attractive container subjects,
spilling over the rim with their bold, heart-shaped
leaves. Here the colours of hosta 'Wide Brim' are
echoed in a soft blue dwarf spruce and the
yellow variegation of a vibrant Japanese spindle.

Planting & care Plant the container at any time of year
using a moisture-retentive compost to which you have
added some extra well-rotted manure or garden compost.
Place in partial shade – some sunshine will maintain the
bright foliage colours, but protect the hosta from the
midday sun. Keep the compost moist at all times because
hostas will not tolerate drought. Fork a little bonemeal or
other slow-release fertilizer into the top of the compost
each spring.

Or you could try a blue and silver display with a blue-
leaved hosta such as 'Blue Moon' or 'Halcyon' and
silver-leaved oleaster (*Elaeagnus* 'Quicksilver') instead
of the spindle.

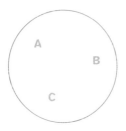

drought-busting basket

You need

1 *Aloe ferox* **A**

1 pink *Echeveria* cultivar **B**

4 *Echeveria elegans* cultivar **C**

2 *Sempervivum tectorum* (houseleek) **D**

1 *Rhodiola pachyclados* **E**

1 *Aeonium* 'Zwartkop' **F**

1 *Graptopetalum* cultivar (crassula) **G**

Succulents are perfect for hanging baskets because they are tolerant of drought, and it is notoriously difficult to keep basket compost moist. Choose a varied selection of different shapes and forms for a fascinating display.

Planting & care Plant the basket at any time of year. Line the wire basket with hessian and fill it with free-draining compost. Plant the succulents in the top and sides of the basket, aiming for a good contrast of shapes and colours. Hang the basket in a sunny, sheltered spot and water from time to time in warm weather. These plants are tender and must be kept at a minimum of 10°C (50°F), so place in a greenhouse or in a sunny window indoors over winter.

Or you could try growing Christmas cacti (*Schlumbergera*) in a hanging basket as the spreading fleshy stems hang down in an attractive manner. These tender plants produce prolific vibrant pink and red flowers in late winter.

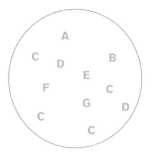

colourful cushions

You need

16 *Sempervivum* cultivars
(houseleek) **A**

A shallow bowl of gritty compost is the perfect place for a collection of houseleeks, which will form colourful cushions of neat rosettes. In summer stems bearing clusters of exotic little blooms appear above the rosettes.

Planting & care Plant the bowl at any time of year using a free-draining compost to which you have added about a third by volume of horticultural grit. Place in a sunny position sheltered from heavy rain, and water only in very dry weather. Remove the old rosettes as they die after flowering, to be replaced by the new rosettes that form around the edges of the clumps. Apply a liquid fertilizer in spring each year.

Or you could try a collection of low-growing succulent stonecrops (*Sedum*), such as *Sedum acre* with fleshy green stems and yellow flowers, *S. humifusum* with its hairy rosettes, *S. obtusatum* with its fat red-tinged foliage and *S. spathulifolium* 'Purpureum' with fleshy rosettes in purple and grey.

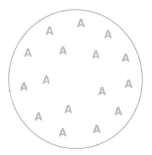

stripy sedges

You need

1 *Anemanthele lessoniana* (pheasant's tail grass) **A**

3 *Carex ornithopoda* 'Variegata' (bird's foot sedge) **B**

3 *Heuchera villosa* 'Palace Purple' (coral flower) **C**

These tall, elegant terracotta pots have been filled with grasses and coral flower in a naturalistic planting in muted shades. The plants enhance the honey-coloured stone wall beside which the pots are standing.

Planting & care Plant the tubs at any time of year using a moisture-retentive compost. Tidy the grasses from time to time by removing any dead stems. Keep the compost moist at all times and fork a little bonemeal or other slow-release fertilizer into the top of the compost each spring.

Or you could try planting a lime green Bowles's golden sedge (*Carex elata* 'Aurea') in the centre of the tub and foam flower (*Tiarella cordifolia*) instead of the purple-leaved coral flower, which is similar in form but has pale green leaves.

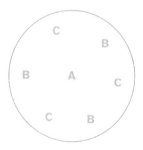

easy and edible

veg in vogue

You need

4 *Pelargonium* 'Lady Plymouth' **A**

4 *Mentha* x *piperita* (peppermint) **B**

4 spinach **C**

Who said the vegetable patch has to be hidden away? This cool and contemporary galvanized tub boasts an elegant mixture of leafy spinach, upright peppermint and frilly-leaved, eucalyptus-scented pelargoniums, which will perfume the air as you brush past.

Planting & care Plant the tub in spring after all risk of frost has passed. Buy the mint and pelargoniums as young plants; spinach can be grown from seed sown in situ. Choose a fertile, moisture-retentive compost and keep it moist to keep the spinach in growth: if it dries out it will go to seed. Harvest the spinach and mint as you need them, picking the outer spinach leaves first. Sow more spinach as necessary.

Or you could try growing perpetual spinach instead. Although the flavour is not quite as good, it is easier to grow, more tolerant of windy or exposed sites and will not go to seed. Sow the seed in mid-spring and start picking as soon as it is large enough.

mediterranean flavours

You need

1 *Santolina chamaecyparissus* (cotton lavender) **A**

1 *Salvia officinalis* 'Purpurascens' (purple sage) **B**

1 *Salvia officinalis* (common sage) **C**

2 scented pelargoniums **D**

2 *Thymus vulgaris* (thyme) **E**

1 *Rosmarinus officinalis* (rosemary) **F**

A white-washed terracotta pot is the perfect foil for a range of Mediterranean herbs, which look as good as they taste. Most of these plants are evergreen, so you can appreciate their decorative and culinary qualities right through the year.

Planting & care Plant the tub in spring when all risk of frost has passed. Choose a free-draining compost and add a little extra grit to improve the drainage even more. Remove the spent blooms from the cotton lavender and sage after flowering. The pelargoniums will die off over winter: remove the plants and replace them with new ones in the spring.

Or you could try other Mediterranean herbs, such as fennel with its feathery foliage and aniseed taste, lemon verbena with its wonderful lemony aroma, or lavender with its beautiful purple flowers instead.

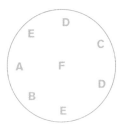

cool kale

You need

4 kale 'Nero di Toscana' **A**

9 *Allium schoenoprasum* (chives) **B**

It's no surprise that kale is coming back into fashion: these handsome, architectural plants are extremely tough and hardy, producing a steady crop of succulent leaves from winter through to spring. Here they are underplanted with chives, another culinary staple.

Planting & care Plant the tub in late spring or summer, choosing a free-draining compost. Be sure to firm the compost well around the roots of the plants. Harvest the chives as you need them, but wait to start harvesting the kale until after the first frosts as the flavour will be better. Choose only the tender young leaves because older leaves will be bitter. Replace the kale with fresh plants each spring or summer.

Or you could try some of the other kale cultivars, such as 'Red Russian' with its feathery red leaves, 'Ragged Jack' with its pink-tinged foliage or 'Redbor', a red curly kale. All are just as attractive.

abundant aromatics

You need

3 alpine strawberries **A**

1 scented pelargonium **B**

1 French lavender **C**

3 yellow variegated sage **D**

1 *Glechoma hederacea* 'Variegata' **E**

2 lemon balm **F**

2 nasturtiums **G**

1 camomile **H**

1 sweet cicely **I**

1 lemongrass **J**

1 white variegated sage **K**

1 French marigold **L**

1 *Nepeta nervosa* (catmint) **M**

1 purple basil **N**

1 chives **O**

1 fennel **P**

1 golden feverfew **Q**

This simple white windowbox is overflowing with herbs of all types. Position it on the kitchen windowsill for a ready supply of aromatics, whatever you are cooking.

Planting & care Plant the windowbox in spring using a range of small herb plants. Use a moisture-retentive compost and add moisture-retaining gel crystals to sustain so many plants in a small space. It is also a good idea to insert fertilizer sticks into the compost to feed the plants. Discard the plants when the annuals die and the herbaceous perennials die back in the winter, and start again with fresh plants the following spring.

Or you could try devoting the windowbox just to your favourite herb, rather than a whole mixture. For example, you could grow a range of different basils, including lemon basil, lime basil, purple basil, Thai basil and 'Sweet Genovese' with tender, sweet green foliage.

C	D	J	O	D	P
B	F	H	I	F	A	N	Q
A	E	G	D	K	L	M	A	G

bountiful beans

You need

4 dwarf French bean
  'Berrgold' **A**

4 lettuce 'Lollo Rossa' **B**

This hanging basket display comprises delicious stringless yellow beans and frilly red lettuces, as appealing to the eye as to the palate. Feed and water well, and both will reward you with a good supply of produce for many weeks in summer.

Planting & care Plant the basket in late spring when all risk of frost has passed. Choose a moisture-retentive compost and add moisture-retaining gel crystals to prevent the compost from drying out. Water every day, twice in very warm weather, and feed once a week. Harvest the beans as they become large enough: the more you pick, the more the plants will produce. These are non-hearting lettuces, so you can pick individual leaves as you need them, and the plants will produce more.

Or you could try combining 'Purple Queen' beans, which have handsome purple pods, with bright green lettuce 'Lollo Bionda' for an equally eye-catching basket.

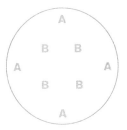

strawberry cocktail

You need

6 alpine strawberries **A**

2 *Borago officinalis* (borage) **B**

2 *Sanguisorba minor* (salad burnet) **C**

Tiny alpine strawberries and cucumber-scented borage are ideal for adding a refreshing taste to summer drinks and cocktails. Here they are planted in a galvanized bucket, together with salad burnet.

Planting & care Plant up the container in late spring using a free-draining, moisture-retentive compost. Make sure there are plenty of drainage holes in the bottom of the bucket. Water regularly and feed once a week to encourage the strawberries to produce fruits. Pick the leaves and strawberries as you need them – they make a delicious and pretty decoration for summer desserts as well as cocktails. Discard the borage plants in the winter and replace with new plants in spring.

Or you could try using mint instead of borage, another favourite ingredient in summer drinks. Choose the pretty variegated pineapple mint (*Mentha suaveolens* 'Variegata'), with its cream- and green-splashed leaves.

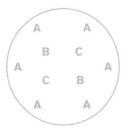

fish-lovers' favourites

You need

2 *Petroselinum crispum*
  (parsley) **A**

2 *Anethum graveolens*
  'Bouquet' (dill) **B**

1 *Artemisia dracunculus*
  (French tarragon) **C**

3 *Thymus citriodorus* 'Golden
  King' (lemon thyme) **D**

2 *Thymus vulgaris* 'Silver
  Posie' (thyme) **E**

This windowbox display is designed for fish-lovers, with all the favourite herbs – parsley, dill, tarragon and thyme – which enhance fish and seafood dishes. Use the leaves in sauces and marinades, or simply sprinkle over your fish on the barbecue.

Planting & care Plant the windowbox in spring using a free-draining compost. Feed and water well for a plentiful supply of foliage throughout the summer. The tarragon and thymes are perennial plants, which can stay in the windowbox year after year. Dill is an annual; it will die off in the autumn and should be replaced with fresh plants in the spring. Parsley is biennial; it will flower and die in its second year, when it should be replaced

Or you could try growing these plants in a trough and stand it next to the barbecue so you have fresh herbs to hand where you need them most.

A	B	C	B	A
D	E	D	E	D

two peas in a pod

You need

6 pea 'Half Pint' **A**

6 *Lathyrus odoratus*
   'Cupid' (sweet pea) **B**

This endearing hanging basket combines decorative, scented sweet peas with real peas – true cottage garden charm. Pick both flowers and peas regularly for a steady supply of both throughout the summer.

Planting & care Plant the basket in late spring when all risk of frost has passed. Use a fertile, moisture-retentive compost, and add some well-rotted manure if possible. Keep the compost moist at all times and feed regularly to keep the flowers and peas coming. Remove the sweet pea flowers as they die to encourage more blooms. Pick the peas as soon as they are large enough – they will be so sweet you won't be able to resist eating them straight from the plant.

Or you could try planting asparagus peas (*Lotus tetragonolobus*) instead. This unusual but highly decorative vegetable has very pretty red flowers and delicious winged pods.

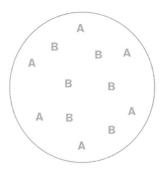

sweet sensation

You need

9 strawberry 'Aromel' **A**

Strawberries growing in a hanging basket are easy to harvest, the precious fruits stay clean and dry, and, perhaps most importantly, the slugs can't reach them. Choose a perpetual variety and you'll be harvesting sweet fruits through summer and autumn.

Planting & care Plant the hanging basket in autumn, with the bases of the crowns level with the surface of the compost. Choose a moisture-retentive compost, to which you have added some extra garden compost and a spinkling of bonemeal. Water and feed regularly in the spring and summer, but avoid wetting the plants' leaves. Remove any runners that appear to preserve the plants' energy. Pick the fruits as they ripen. In autumn cut off the old foliage and apply a balanced fertilizer.

Or you could try growing a summer-fruiting variety rather than a perpetual strawberry, for a larger summer crop. Try 'Hapil' or 'Cambridge Favourite'.

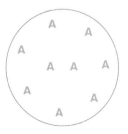

tumbling tomatoes

You need

2 *Petroselinum crispum* (parsley) **A**

2 *Thunbergia alata* (black-eyed Susan) **B**

2 tomato 'Tumbling Tom Red' **C**

2 tomato 'Tumbling Tom Yellow' **D**

A vibrant mixture of red and yellow tomatoes, curly parsley and black-eyed Susan makes a fine display for a hanging basket. These bushy little tomato plants produce masses of juicy, cherry-sized fruits from summer to autumn.

Planting & care Plant up the basket in late spring when all risk of frost has passed. Use rich, moisture-retentive compost, to which you have added some water-retaining gel crystals. Line the basket with polythene to retain moisture. Feed and water regularly as the plants are growing. Water consistently when the fruits appear: erratic watering can cause them to split. Pick the parsley as you need it, and harvest the tomatoes as they ripen. Discard the plants in autumn.

Or you could try growing chillies or peppers in the basket instead of the tomatoes. Choose compact, bushy varieties, such as pepper 'Minimix', which produces lots of little peppers in shades of red, orange and green; or chilli 'Prairie Fire' which will be covered in mini red chillies with a hot, fiery flavour.

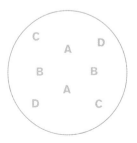

index

acknowledgements

Publisher Jane Birch
Managing editor Clare Churly
Design manager Tokiko Morishima
Designer Ginny Zeal
Picture library assistant Ciaran O'Reilly
Senior production controller Manjit Sihra

photography

Alamy Holmes Garden Photos 46; Keith Mindham 203; Mark Bolton Photography 69;

Andrew Lawson Andrew Lawson 51, 51, 52, 53, 143, 153, 155, 157; Paul Williams 211; Powis Castle 148;

Clive Nichols Clive Nichols 55, 61, 92, 107, 130, 139;

Gap Photos Elke Borkowski 75; FhF Greenmedia 199; Francois De Heel 149; Friedrich Strauss 58, 67, 73, 85, 88, 115, 129, 158, 167; Graham Strong 29, 31, 35, 41, 91, 95, 125, 135, 161, 173, 183, 185, 205, 207, 223; Howard Rice 27; J S Sira 113, 215; Jerry Harpur 189, 217; John Glover 221; Mark Bolton 99; Richard Bloom 187, 201;

GardenPhotoLibrary Derek St. Romaine 219;

Harpur Garden Library Jerry Harpur 133; Marcus Harpur 25, 175, 177, 193;

Marianne Majerus 45;

Octopus Publishing Group Limited 144; Diana Beddoes 137; Freia Turland 8, 10, 13, 14, 16, 18, 18, 21, 140, 212, 225, 227, 229, 231, 233; Mark Bolton 82, 82;

Photolibrary Claire Davies 121; Graham Strong 22, 43, 65; Howard Rice 49, 71; John Glover 165, 179; Lynne Brotchie 181;

Photoshot Michael Warren 87, 103;

The Garden Collection Andrew Lawson 33, 37, 57, 81, 111, 119, 171; Derek Harris 77, 79; Liz Eddison 39, 97, 101, 109, 117, 123, 162, 163, 197; Marie O' Hara 127, 190, 195, 209; Nicola Stocken Tomkins 63, 105, 147